PERSPECTIVES ON CARIBBEAN FOOTBALL

PERSPECTIVES ON CARIBBEAN FOOTBALL

Christopher A.D. Charles

Editor

Published by Hansib Publications, 2015

Hansib Publications Limited
P.O. Box 226, Hertford, Hertfordshire, SG14 3WY
United Kingdom
info@hansibpublications.com

www.hansibpublications.com

ISBN 978-1-910553-08-4

A CIP catalogue record for this book
is available from the British Library.

Production
Hansib Publications Limited

Printed in Great Britain.

To the memory of Moses Murray

Contents

Acronyms & Abbreviations

CARICOM
    Caribbean Community
CBO
    Community Based Organisations
CONCACAF
    Confederation of North, Central American, and Caribbean
    Football Association
CFU
    Caribbean Football Union
FA
    Football Associations
FIFA
    Fédération Internationale de Football Association
GAT
    Greater August Town
IFAD
    International Fund for Agricultural Development
JSLC
    Jamaica Survey of Living Conditions
JWFA
    Jamaica Women's Football Association
KSAFA
    Kingston and St Andrew Football Association
NPL
    National Premier League
OECS
    Organisation of Eastern Caribbean States
SIDs
    Small Island Developing States
UPP
    Pacifying Police Unit
UWI
    University of the West Indies

List of Illustrations

Foreword

When I was asked to write the foreword for this book, it came as a big surprise. At 87 years old my memory is not too good; no, bad!!! Anyhow, I will do my best. The authors have taken on a mammoth task, and have given me one. I took it on with the seriousness with which I played professional football in England.

People in the Commonwealth Caribbean have always excelled in many sports, mainly athletics, cricket, netball and football. My subject on this occasion is football. We are certainly not the leaders but we have made contributions to international football. In the region, John Barnes, Gil Heron, Allan Cole, Dwight Yorke, Russell Latapy, Stern John, Shaka Hislop, Ricardo Gardener, Ricardo Fuller and yours truly among others have made their contributions.

I will make special mention of myself, Heron and Barnes who made it very big in the leading football country in the world, England, in the 1940s, 1950s and 1980s respectively. The three of us all made the grade in those years. Heron played for Ayr United in Scotland, Barnes for Liverpool and England and yours truly for Portsmouth the 1st Division Champion in 1947 and 1948 for which I got the 1st division medal and Middlesborough 1st division from 1952-1957.

Barnes, Heron and I went from the tiny Caribbean region, where people outside the region thought we lived in trees, to play excellent football in the top professional league in the world at the time. I almost replaced Stanley Mathews in the 1954 England team when he suffered an injury. However, John Barnes played for England decades later.

In more recent times Raheem Sterling and Daniel Sturridge of Liverpool came to the fore and played for England in the 2014 World Cup in Brazil. Others from the English-speaking Caribbean such as Dwight Yorke, Russell Latapy, Stern John, Shaka Hislop, Ricardo Gardener, and Ricardo Fuller played professionally in England and elsewhere. These are players from the Caribbean who made it to the zenith of sports, professional football. Some people will disagree with me but that's life. I wouldn't compare the Caribbean players of the 1940s and 1950s with those from the 1980s to the present. It would be unfair because of changes in the game of football and the changes in equipment and gear. The authors have taken on a colossal task in this book and you will definitely enjoy it like I did!

Lindy Delapenha
Former Professional Footballer in the English First Division
January 2015, Kingston

Acknowledgement

The writing of this book would not have been possible without the contribution of many people. The first Academic Conference on International Football held at the University of the West Indies (UWI) was the brainchild of Don Davis during his doctoral studies in the Institute of Caribbean Studies, at the UWI. The conference received monetary support from Donna Hope-Marquis, the head of the Institute of Caribbean Studies, for which I am grateful. Support from the institute was also evident in the yeowoman's service given by Cultural Studies graduate student Trojean Burrell who worked tirelessly on the planning and running of the conference.

The head of the Department of Government, Lloyd Waller, gave immediate support when I told him we wanted to host the football conference. The forward-thinking and astute Lloyd Waller refused to be outperformed so the Department of Government matched the monetary contribution of the Institute of Caribbean Studies thus providing sufficient funds not only to host the conference but also for the publication of the book. Thanks also to the administrative officer in the Department of Government, June Pinto, and my research assistant, Sania Brown, for their support of the conference.

I would also like to acknowledge and say thank you to the dean of the Faculty of Social Sciences, Evan Duggan, and the dean of the Faculty of Humanities, Swithin Wilmot, for their support of the conference and this book. A special thank you to Professor Carolyn Cooper and the roundtable presenters, especially those who came at short notice - Lascelve Graham, Clyde Jureidini, Charles Edwards, Tony James, Allan Cole and Trevor 'Jumpy' Harris among others. Thanks are also extended to the chairpersons of the roundtables and academic panels – Osayimwese Osagboro, Afifa Harris, Winston Campbell, Bail Wilson, Imani Tafari-Ama, Jahlani Niaah, Don Davis and Dennis Howard.

This book would not be possible without the academic presenters who each agreed to submit a chapter and who worked assiduously to complete their chapters by the deadline. I am also grateful for their calm responses to the many phone calls and emails reminding them of the various deadlines. Special thanks to the keynote speaker at the conference Emeritus Professor of Psychiatry Frederick Hickling who submitted a chapter based on his speech. Thanks also to Tony Talburt who agreed to contribute a chapter although he did not present at the conference. The peer reviewers of the chapters elevated the quality of the book with their comments.

I am also greatly indebted to Sean Mock Yen from the University Archives who did the audio recording of the conference proceedings. My research assistant, Tsashana Thompson transcribed the academic presentations which greatly assisted several of the contributors in this book. It would be remiss of me not to mention the conference attendees whose participation enriched the discourse and the information in the book.

Introduction

Christopher A.D. Charles

The people of the Caribbean are passionate about football. The passion among fans comes from the nature of the game, its dynamics and the difficulty and fight to score. The uncertain moments in the game can cause fans to become passionately upset and anxious (Clanche, 1998). This beautiful game, which evokes such strong emotions, has not received much scholarly attention in the Caribbean. I, therefore, thought it was important to create something special by exploiting the passion shared by football practitioners and several academics by bringing them together to interrogate Caribbean football. This book is the outcome.

The book focuses on the state of football in the Caribbean, the obstacles and opportunities that are linked to the growth of the sport, the need for a football philosophy of play in the region that reflects each Caribbean country's ethos and style of the game backed by resources and a scientific approach. These, it is argued, are required for Caribbean countries to play football at the highest level, as we do in the sports of netball, track and field and cricket. If success is to be achieved the issues of gender, culture, identity, history, philosophy, social structures and community development must be taken into account.

The independent Anglophone micro-states that lie in the Caribbean Sea and Guyana – the Caribbean Community (CARICOM) of six million people – are the countries which this book deals with. CARICOM has a shared history of plantation slavery, and colonialism under British rule and the failed West Indian Federation, political independence (with Westminster constitutions) and persistent poverty (Beckford, 2000; Girvan, 2001; Knight & Palmer, 1989; Philips, 1985; Time for Action, 1993). These developing countries are stable, two-party dominant democracies with small economies. The economies are dependent on tourism and primary exports of mined natural resources and agriculture, and manufacturing in a few states, as well as aid, and grants from friendly governments, and loans from international financial agencies (Beckford, 2000; Braveboy-Wagner, 1993; Girvan, 2001; Knight & Palmer, 1989). The income of these states varies widely. According to the World Development Report (2010) there are: two low middle income countries (Guyana and Jamaica); eight upper middle income countries (Belize, Dominica, Grenada, St Kitts and Nevis, Montserrat, St Lucia and St Vincent and the Grenadines); and four high income countries (Antigua and Barbuda, The Bahamas, Barbados, and Trinidad and Tobago). The countries of Haiti and Suriname are now members of CARICOM but they do not have the shared colonial history of British rule, and British political and legal systems. These relatively new members of CARICOM and observer country Cuba are excluded from any detailed discussion since the book focuses on the Anglophone Caribbean.

The English not only exploited its colonies in the Caribbean but also introduced the people to the game of football. The colonies were sites of exploitation rather than development so when the professional football league started in England this professionalism wasn't diffused to the Caribbean. Football in the Caribbean is developing like the dependent economies of the region (Wagner, 1982).

The various Caribbean countries have local football federations which are affiliated with Fédération Internationale de Football Association (FIFA). These federations follow the rules of FIFA in local football competitions. Only Trinidad and Tobago and Jamaica have high school football competitions. Many Caribbean countries field national teams for the Caribbean Cup competition hosted annually by the Caribbean Football Union (CFU) which was established in 1978. The CFU also hosts the CFU club championships and the men's and women's under-17 and under-20 competitions. The CFU has 31members in the union which includes countries from the English, French, Spanish and Dutch Caribbean.

The Caribbean is a part of FIFA's Confederation of North, Central American, and Caribbean Football Association (CONCACAF) which has 41 members. CONCACAF hosts the under-15, the under-17 and the under-20 competitions as well as the Gold Cup, the Olympic Qualifying, the Champions League, the Central American Cup, and the Futsal and Beach football competitions. The presence of CFU and

CONCACAF demonstrates that the countries of the Commonwealth Caribbean have regional and international competitions that they can participate in but they first have to efficiently organise their local football competitions and raise their standard of play so that they can consistently perform at the top of these competitions. Despite the fact that the standard of football in CONCACAF is relatively low compared to the standard of play in some of the other FIFA regional associations, some footballers from the Caribbean play professionally in the United States and Europe (Ferguson, 2006; Kuethe & Motamed, 2010).

The demonstration of the love and passion for football in the Caribbean reaches its zenith during the FIFA World Cup competition every four years. People in the region display strong public support for the football teams of countries like Brazil, Argentina, Germany, France, England, Holland, Spain, Portugal, Nigeria and Ghana. For example, in the FIFA 2014 World Cup competition many people in St Vincent and the Grenadines met at Heritage Square in Kingstown to cheer their favourite World Cup team, some wearing the team jerseys. Some Jamaicans also wore the jerseys of their favourite teams but many more walked with the flags of the countries whose team they were supporting or mounted these flags on their motor vehicles. In Trinidad and Tobago and Jamaica there were also meeting places for football fans to watch the 2014 World Cup. The passion people have for the game in the region has not morphed into consistently high quality performance of Caribbean football teams at the international level.

Only two Commonwealth Caribbean countries have qualified for the World Cup, Jamaica in 1998, and Trinidad and Tobago in 2006. Jamaica, in 1998, lost 3-1 to Croatia, 5-0 to Argentina but defeated Japan 2-1. In 2006, Trinidad and Tobago drew 0-0 with Sweden, but they were defeated 2-0 by England, and Paraguay. The other countries in the wider Caribbean to qualify for the World Cup were Cuba in 1938 and Haiti in 1974. Despite the qualification of Trinidad and Tobago and Jamaica for the World Cup, these countries and others continue to struggle to reach subsequent World Cups.

Moving beyond the sphere of competition, football is a force for Caribbean regional integration and identity because some footballers that were born in Britain of Caribbean parents wanted to be a part of the Jamaican World Cup Reggae Boys team in Paris in 1998 (Howe, 1998). Relatedly, the Caribbean nationals that descended on Paris to support Jamaica put on parties that blared Caribbean music (Tomlinson, 2007). Guinto (2009) argues that football which unifies people around the world is also a unifying force in strife-torn Haiti, in particular, and the Caribbean in general. The love for the game is also very evident in the Caribbean Diaspora because Caribbean nationals create amateur football teams and competitions in Britain, Canada and the United States. These Caribbean nationals are emotionally attached to the game which gives meaning and purpose to their lives (Burdsey, 2009; Campbell, 2014; Marcus, 2009; Walter, Brown & Grabb, 1991).

The love for football in the Caribbean and the importance of the game to the region influenced the writing of this book. Most of the chapters in the book are based on some of the papers presented at the Inaugural Academic Conference on International Football held at the UWI, Mona, April 16-17, 2014. The information provided in the chapters deconstructs the problem of football in terms of power and social structures, culture and community development, gender inequality, poverty, history, strategy of play, philosophy, nationalism and the Diaspora, World Cup lessons, and the psychology of football and the need for professionalism. The book ends with some ideas to bring the standard of Caribbean football to international standard.

Chapter 1 of the book provides a sociological treatise of football and sets the theoretical background for the book. The chapter examines the sociology of football which began out of the historicity of European society where football began as an elitist game and spread like British colonialism to all parts of the globe. The chapter shows how the game of football and its colonial spread mirrors the sociology of different periods. Football became the intersecting trajectories of race, class, colour, politics, culture and identity. Conflict and other sociological perspectives were used to examine the game as an arena of contestation within the social construction of people's realities in the Caribbean. Football became part of the dialectic that propels social change, whether good or bad, in society and especially among and within communities. The game also became more of an arena of conflict and integration when it became part of the contradictions and conflict within Caribbean societies.

The second chapter, which interrogates gender in football, comes from a shortened M.A. thesis. The chapter examines the coercive influences of hegemonic masculinity through the lens of football. Male hegemony influences norms that dictate the different ways in which men and women are treated in society. This differential treatment is evident in football. Journalists argued that male football competitions receive more media coverage than female football competitions because the former receives more sponsorship from the private sector. Many spectators believe that the skills of women footballers are inferior to that of men, so they give the female games lower ratings. If a woman plays very well during a game she is viewed as a man. Moreover, these spectators believe that women should not play football, because it is a dangerous man's game. Therefore, women who play football must be lesbians. Football reflects the gender stereotypes and inequalities in the society.

The role of football and culture in community development is the focus of chapter 3. The Greater August Town (GAT) community in Jamaica has had a long relationship with football and a sense of community. Football has tempered episodes of violence and brought warring factions onto neutral grounds and encouraged people to form associations beyond borders and break the community divide. Football has been seen as an intervention strategy capable of stabilising communities. The work of Mona Social Services illustrates how football has fostered development of shared values and beliefs across community corners. The chapter highlights how these shared values and beliefs transformed community spaces into multi-purpose, neutral settings. The chapter utilises qualitative techniques to reveal how the way of life in GAT is improved during periods of football engagement and the creation of spaces represents people integrating by moving across traditional borders. The findings indicate that there is a positive relationship between football engagement and constructive ways of life in GAT. However, community football has not been given latitude to be economically viable and become a catalyst for cultural tourism.

Chapter 4 explores what the Caribbean can learn from the social protests in Brazil related to the 2014 World Cup. Brazil's rise as a world power in football is now matched by the government's quest for the country to be recognised as a global power. Mass protests erupted during the Confederation Cup as workers protested the cost of holding the World Cup, the cost overruns, and the neglect of human capital in the favelas. The Brazilian football team also performed poorly at the World Cup which added insult to injury. Countries host international sporting events to heighten their prestige on the world stage but the cost of the games left Brazil a deeply fractured society, wrestling with the fissures of inequality which threaten social order. The Caribbean states in thinking about economic development should take note that it should be embrace marginalised groups. Popular leaders who take the marginalised into account are needed during the process of change. Social protests will be triggered if the changes in the society occur without building social capital between the people and governmental institutions. Finally, the governments leading the transformation must be able to navigate globalisation successfully.

The focus of chapter 5 is the British Guianese football genius Andrew Watson (1856-1921). The Caribbean has not seen the level of success in football as we have had in cricket and track and field. The region is not known for its ability to produce many footballers of a high international standard who can be considered household names. Alan Skill Cole who played for the top Brazilian Club Nautica, Dwight Yorke who played for Manchester United and Lindy Delapenha who played for Portsmouth, Middlesborough, Mansfield and Burton Albion, among others, are exceptions to the rule. Given this situation, it might at first seem ironic that this chapter seeks to examine the achievements of one Caribbean-born footballer whose on and off the field ability was truly remarkable. The chapter begins by providing a biographical overview of Watson before examining the significance of the period in which he played and the teams for which he played.

Watson not only played football in England and Scotland in the 1870s and 1880s, and was probably the world's first Black footballer, but he was almost certainly the world's first Black national football captain. What is even more remarkable is that Watson played and captained the Scottish national football team in 1881 at a time when Scotland was arguably the very best national team in the world. The chapter examines the remarkable achievements of this Caribbean-born football genius who was one of the world's greatest players and also one of the early pioneers who contributed to the development of the modern game of football.

Chapter 6 looks at how the misuse of scrimmage in the Caribbean destroys the game. Scrimmage is useful for developing certain footballing skills as a part of a larger development programme. However, this is not the case in the Caribbean because many people's first introduction to the game is through scrimmage in a small space which is not tied to a structured trajectory of growth. Scrimmage as it is used in the Caribbean leads to the underdevelopment of: (1) goal keepers because the players standing in the goal can't use his or her hands; (2) strikers because they do not have big goals to shoot at; (3) headers of the ball or players who can trap the ball on their chests because these situations hardly occurs in games of scrimmage; and (4) corner takers and proper throwers of the ball because the pitch is too small. Footballers socialised in scrimmage games are lost when they play on the right-sized pitch. These players do not play well because they do not know how to properly receive the ball and run off the ball and the roles of their positions and their relationships to other playing positions because these cannot be learnt in the confines of the small spaces used for scrimmage. The strategy of play needs to change and develop in the Caribbean where youngsters are always taught to play the game on the right-sized pitch and scrimmage is only used to develop selected skills.

The essence of chapter 7 is that playing excellent football requires the development of a football philosophy and Jamaica is used as the site of discussion. Since Jamaica's qualification for the 1998 World Cup in France, the national teams have struggled to qualify for subsequent World Cups. Attempts at qualification for the Olympics have been dismal, so too the Gold Cup. The JFF has invested in the notion that Jamaica's success lies in hiring foreign coaches. Some people have argued that it is the lack of a football philosophy that has created the haphazard and disjointed development of football at the national level. The chapter traces the hiring of foreign coaches starting with Tassy and others with the noted success of René Simões. The discussion also looks at how effective the use of overseas coaches has been and concludes that the lack of a Jamaican football philosophy has contributed to an ineffective national programme and mediocre national teams.

In chapter 8 it is argued that Jamaica's qualification for the 1998 World Cup in France was a momentous occasion in Jamaica's history. The chapter subsequently applies Bruce Tuckman's famous model of group development *forming*, *storming*, *norming*, *performing*, and *adjourning* to explain how Jamaica's World Cup team developed and performed using secondary data. The chapter goes on to discuss how the World Cup campaign connected Jamaicans at home and abroad (the Diaspora) along with other Caribbean nationals that celebrated Jamaica's achievement. The chapter ends with lessons for the Caribbean such as how to select players (local versus overseas), the need for strong, decisive, influential and effective leadership in football, the importance of the Diaspora in national development, the crucial nexus between music and sports, the need for a sustained presence in international football and the importance of football as a mechanism for regional integration.

Chapter 9 outlines the clinical experience of a Jamaican psychiatrist in relation to mental disorders and sports, mental disorders and management, and the development and application of mental skills. It is argued that the development and application of these skills will enhance the personal growth of the athletes and improve their performance so that they can move from excellent local play to extraordinary international play. The chapter presents four clinical case studies and their resolutions that demonstrate the problematic relationship between psychiatry and football in Jamaica within the context that approximately 70 per cent of Jamaicans will experience at least one mental disorder at some time during the course of their lives. The chapter argues, further, that psychiatrists and psychologists should be integrated into football teams in conjunction with the effective organisation of sporting talent. This critically crucial partnership will lead to individual, team and national transformation through exceptional performances.

The brief discourse in chapter 10 comes from the integration of ideas from the previous chapters of the book and the vibrant, insightful and often contentious arguments at the conference. The chapter suggests a future path for Caribbean football by making football a business in the region, the development of local coaches, development of a football philosophy in the various countries, and the development of a unique style of play. Other strategies in the service of the future are: the creation of long-term integrated football development programmes; the provision of pipelines to move from local to international play; the establishment of integrated technical teams, and the development of participatory governance structures. Finally, it is useful to use football to improve academic learning, promote community development and gender equality.

In this book the term Reggae Boys is used instead of Reggae Boyz. The book ultimately argues that the beloved football reflects societal cleavages but it also brings people together. The ethos of cooperation and identity that football engenders means that it is a useful tool to promote gender equality and community development. This development should be a part of the macro-economic development in Caribbean countries that includes vulnerable citizens. Development without a human face will lead to protest about the money spent on football and other sports. The Caribbean has a rich footballing history because British Guianese footballer Andrew Watson was one of the greatest players to grace the modern game. The Caribbean has not produced many Watsons because the misuse of scrimmage is destroying footballing skills that are made worse by the absence of a Caribbean football philosophy and an effective unique style and strategy of play. The foregoing is why Jamaica and Trinidad and Tobago have failed to qualify for the World Cup since their respective debuts in 1998 and 2006. The way forward is the professionalisation of Caribbean football so that countries will be able to bridge the gap between local and international play.

Chapter 1

The Sociology of Football in the Caribbean

Orville W. Beckford

This chapter uses sociology to examine football in the Caribbean and provides a useful background for the later chapters. Wright-Mills (1959) in his *Sociological Imagination* sought to reconcile the individual and society by including the historical dimension whose sensibility can help us to understand our present social realities. I begin by looking at how the history of football has shaped the sports today, which is in keeping with Mills' sociological imagination. Operationally, the sociological imagination highlights the importance of history as a guide to understanding contemporary society's many socio-economic challenges. The sport of football is no different in its historical trajectory. A sport is seen as an expressive part of any society's culture. Like most cultural elements, the culture can be passed from one society to the next by force or acculturation.

Football began in other countries before the 1800s as it did in Britain. Not much historicity is available about the early beginnings of the game. This is not unusual within the imperialism of history where non-Western accounts are not fully represented without much lacuna of its historicity. However, it is interesting to note the earlier existence of the sport in other parts of the world. The FIFA (2014a) notes:

> The very earliest form of the game for which there is scientific evidence was an exercise from a military manual dating back to the second and third centuries BC in China.

> This Han Dynasty forebear of football was called Tsu' Chu and it consisted of kicking a leather ball filled with feathers and hair through an opening, measuring only 30-40cm in width, into a small net fixed onto long bamboo canes. According to one variation of this exercise, the player was not permitted to aim at his target unimpeded, but had to use his

feet, chest, back and shoulders while trying to withstand the attacks of his opponents. Use of the hands was not permitted. Another form of the game, also originating from the Far East, was the Japanese Kemari, which began some 500-600 years later and is still played today. This is a sport lacking the competitive element of Tsu' Chu with no struggle for possession involved. Standing in a circle, the players had to pass the ball to each other, in a relatively small space, trying not to let it touch the ground.

It is not clear as to how the conclusion was drawn that the game started in Great Britain in the 1800s given the antecedents of origins in other places. But, the West is the originator or repository of all good things that form civilisation! Or is it? How important is the history of the period that saw the greatest movement of wealth from the South to the North? The origin and expansion of football in England and Europe took place at a time when the main mode of production was plantation slavery. The period also saw the emergence of industrial society which ushered in capitalism and its many exploitative definitions of work. Hence, in spite of FIFA identifying the origin of football being played in non-Western regions of the world, Great Britain was identified as the country of origin in 1800 AD. The historiography of the sport of football then follows a materialistic path that patterned the rise of capitalism and the economic determinism of society espoused by Marx. It was during this period that Andrew Watson of British Guiana (chapter 5) dazzled Scotland and England with his footballing skills.

Macionis and Plummer (2008, 102) note that "Marx contended that one specific institution – the economy – dominates all others when it comes to steering the direction of society." Marx went on to show how all the social institutions extend economic principles into other areas of life. The emergence of the Football Associations (FA) in England in 1863 was formed initially to promote the love of the sport and to introduce its rules. This seemingly social sport's association would eventually be influenced by economic factors which would become the heart of how the club operates. According to the FA (2014) official web site:

Ebenezer Morley, a London solicitor who formed Barnes FC in 1862, could be called the 'father' of The Association. He wasn't a public school man but old boys from several public schools joined his club and there were 'feverish' disputes about the way the game should be played. Morley wrote to Bell's Life, a popular newspaper, suggesting that football should have a set of rules in the same way that the MCC had them for cricket. His letter led to the first historic meeting at the Freemasons' Tavern in Great Queen Street, near to where Holborn tube station is now.

Rules were seen by the functionalists as helping to create uniformity and would eventually lead to social order. Exactly whose social order or as determined by whom is still a site of contestation between the Marxists and the functionalists. One can see the importance of rules to a game being played on the field of football. It presents both sides with some perception of equity in the administration of the rules both by the referees and the larger football association under whose administration and management the competition is organised. The rules of the game are the most visible of all the regulations associated with the game. These are known by most of the spectators and other adherents of the sport. A bad or missed application of any rule is met with sudden disapproval by one section of the crowd in the same way a good/skilful play by any player would attract spontaneous applause or collective comment.

Does the same visibility apply to other rules governing teams: their social positions in the league; how their players are treated by the league; the application of sanctions; the overarching capitalistic influence of money, power, and politics; and race? The social invisibility of these other rules belies the many other social factors that quietly influence the game and the profits to be made from this social and competitive endeavour called football. Herein lies the etiology of football's procrustean ability to integrate as well as to create conflicts. Even at the community level, where there appears to be an absence of much economic gain or largesse, the game still appears to have similar effects on both sets of players and the community.

The Marxists regard rules as being part of the social control used by the bourgeoisie to elicit more profit and increased domination of the working class. How then does a football competition, organised at the community level by non-bourgeois individuals or by individuals at the subsistence level, manifest these same capitalistic characteristics? Does the presence of social gains transform both individuals and game into the dialectics necessary and amenable to Marx's economic determinism of the capitalist system? The key here is to look at the objectives of the game. Football games are, at face value, competitive sports. But these games consist of rules, regulations, and different groups of individuals with varying expectations about the outcome of the game. These expectations can vary from purely economic gain to altruistic ones. Within that mix of expectations are political, racial and ethnic objectives. These varying social objectives become the catalysts for transforming the different groups into creating super structures of values and belief systems which they will use to judge the outcome of the game.

Football is also a social arbiter in community and society. It becomes the language of cooperation and in some cases division. The flexibility of the social roles of the sport is directly related to the social environment of the community and the wider country. Football can be an engine of integration for communities but it can also be the spark that ignites violence and mayhem if the social combustibles of conflict and underlining social and political tensions crash into each other. The spark can be spontaneous or it can be the result of a seething clash of socio-political forces that have been fed by the embers of social, political and economic tensions. The community can be both the benefactor and victim of the game of football, whether organised at the levels of the corner league, major league, secondary school or national team. The common factors in all these cases are the many different human and social relationships that have to successfully contend and survive the 90 minutes of the game, the length of the season or the socio-political forces that intersect in the most difficult domain of human relationships. Within any sphere of life human relations are, at best, difficult (Beckford, 2009). Football as a game is not only physical but also emotional and social. Herein lies the dilemma at the community level; what is the role of the community in influencing the game? Do communities characterised mainly by the lumpen with their alternative government structures (Charles & Beckford, 2012) have more emotional, economic and political embers to fan the flame of conflict or to fuel the fire of integration in a football competition, whether formal or informal? The structure of some low-income communities found in the Caribbean, and the world over, need closer examination to show the nexus between football as an integrative or conflicting agent of community development.

The Sport of Football, Communities and Social Problems

The focus of analysis in this section will concentrate mainly on the Caribbean. Many communities in which football is played in the Caribbean share similar socio-political problems. The shared history of the region coupled with the contemporary forces of globalisation and neo-liberalism have provided the genesis for the conflation of social problems facing Caribbean communities. Historical factors such as colonialism, slavery, plantation society, indentureship, imperialism, the rise of capitalism in Europe and the subsequent under-development of the Caribbean region, have all contributed to the myriad of social problems that the region now faces at the community level. While some of these historical factors have influenced the birth of globalisation, the resulting integrated and interdependent world has fuelled a host of problems for Caribbean countries and the game of football. At the level of the lowest social denominator these problems are felt and magnified in communities of the Caribbean.

The nature of on-going community development coupled with developments in the wider social world of country and region affects the types of social problems that surface at the community level and affect our approaches to solving these problems. Sports are used very often as the galvanising agent for communities in conflict. The basis for the choice of sports for community integration is the pull effect of sports that draw many different individuals and groups together far beyond the duration of the sporting event. Communities in the contemporary Caribbean face complex problems that require new approaches by both policy makers and community action groups. The game of football at the community level is organised and played in various competitions amidst the plethora of complex social problems existing concurrently within the community. The escalating nadir and decadence that social problems such as crime and violence have caused in some urban communities of the Caribbean also affect the lives of individuals involved in the sport of football, as well as the game itself, and how it is played and perceived by the various actors involved. In addition, many social ills that afflict citizens and communities will concomitantly affect the sport of football at the individual and community levels and the actual game itself. Some of these socioeconomic factors include poverty, unemployment, social inequality, lack of educational opportunities, absent fathers, urbanisation and sexual discrimination. The perception and treatment of the game of football within communities will continue to be influenced by these social ills for as long they remain an integral part of Caribbean societies and entrenched at the community level. The constellation of these social ills leads to negative behaviours among some footballers that require psychiatric intervention to improve personal and team performance. These issues are addressed in chapter 9.

Policy makers continue to approach these problems by starting and focusing on the individuals/groups in the community who they think are the causes of the problems, rather than looking at the problem organically. Unfortunately, the game of football within communities fall victim to this type of thinking. This lack of a sociological approach limits the ability of the problem solvers to see the forest that exists and grows beyond the trees. The organic nature of society requires an approach to problem solving that sees the society as an organic whole with a set of interrelated and interdependent parts that function together. But, this is not the approach of Caribbean governments with meagre resources and consequent myopic views of community development that consistently seek to present short-term gains and political mileage. The organic approach to problem solving should also be applied to the management of the game of football at the national and community levels in the Caribbean. Football management at the community levels in many countries suffer from a lack of government-sponsored and maintained football fields in each community. Youngsters, therefore, play scrimmage in very small spaces that prevent the development of the football skills required for the standard field. Chapter 6 elaborates on this problem.

Creating a New Paradigm for Examining Social Problems Affecting Football at the Community Level

Contemporary social problems are constantly being analysed using the individual as the unit of analysis. This concentration on the individual as the unit of analysis ignores the 'social' in social problems. According to Macionis and Plummer (2002), social issues must involve more than one person. Although a particular action may be carried out by one individual, the interconnectedness and interdependence of our modern society result in actions of one individual affecting the harmony and equilibrium of the whole society. This interdependence is why, from a sociological standpoint, policy making that addresses deviance and other social problems should begin with the larger society which may be responsible for influencing the individual and communities to become involved in such behaviour. The community member at a football game is a composite social being with influences on his/her behaviour coming from all levels of the social structure. The behaviour of government and their real or imagined proxies, who are allowed to set-up alternative government structures, have the largest influence in determining whether the football game will serve as a source of unity or division within a given community.

Simon (1995, 12) notes that there are three basic units of analysis in sociological research "(1) the conservative focus on individual personalities, (2) liberal focus on immediate environments, and (3) a larger (macro) sociological environment, which include both cultural values and larger sociological units such as the nation-state, the political economy, and groups of nations". This approach is needed in solving social problems in the region. We need to move away from the monolithic approach of focusing on the individual or on individual communities which further exacerbates the political divide and stereotyping of certain communities as the genesis for certain social problems. In this regard, the game of football, along with other sports, reflects the stereotyping and profiling of inner-city communities even before a ball is kicked since football is also the most popular sport among the working poor.

The time has come for Caribbean communities to make concerted attempts to abandon this feature of plantation society which Beckford (1999, 7) describes as: "A strong individualism that contributes more to clashes of interest in interpersonal relations than cooperative activity". The game of football can be seen as having cooperative activities involving the entire community. The display of individual skills lends excitement to the game but the roar of approval from the community crowd attending a competitive game between teams from two warring communities from the same area is a refulgent point of community integration. The high individualism which characterises contemporary Caribbean society has socialised policy makers and community members alike into paying attention to matters relating to their individual objectives, gains or satisfaction, rather than focusing on the goals and needs of the wider society and/or the community. As a result, there is a reductionist approach to social problems, where the problem solvers believe that the focus on a narrow band of individuals and social issues will provide solutions to the myriad intractable problems facing the society. The game of football can serve as a metaphor in this regard. If the community and coach focus on just the star players and how they affect the game then the needs of the community and spectators will be lost in the sea of individuation which can so easily become friable. The needs of the entire community should supersede that of narrow self-interests that are relying on the actual outcome of the game whose results may be more divisive for the community. Geo and Noonan (2007) highlight the role of competition in affecting the structure of community in North America. For Berry and Kasarda (1977) it is best to focus on the role of interdependencies in community survival and de-emphasise competition in the process.

The interdependencies among communities are not features of small state politics. The politics is extremely divisive in places such as Guyana, Trinidad and Tobago and Jamaica. So much is at stake due to the level of poverty and social dependency on the state. In Jamaica the political culture has split communities into highly polarised garrisons where politics touches everything, including sports. The organisation and execution of small corner league competitions involving six football teams can result in such cabal political subterfuge that police have to be present at all matches to save spectators, players and officials from irascible behaviour. The spoils of the day do not have to be monetary gain; bragging rights sometimes carry more emotional division than money. Therefore, in Caribbean communities that are engaged in violent conflicts it is foolhardy to ask football teams from the warring communities to participate in a peace match since the competition reinforces the divisions between the communities. The best approach for peace is to form a team from the two warring communities so that the team and community members will work towards a common goal of defeating other community football teams, thereby building unity.

In Jamaica, sports is used as an integrative tool to unite the nation and communities. Chapter 3 addresses this issue in greater detail. Although people may have different opinions about a sport issue, the overall effect is somewhat dialectic because in the end it still serves as a point of unity at the dinner table or at the street corner when used to form interdependencies. The nature of the political system has historically been one of the major factors that set communities apart. The complexity of social analysis of community development and sports is enhanced by the fact that all the aforementioned factors can be at play during the execution of a football competition. However, this is not unique to Jamaica and the Caribbean. Burdsey and Chappell(2003,1) show how long-standing differences between religious Protestants and Catholics in both Scotland and Northern Ireland continue to operate within the social processes of sports that shape social identities and the need for social analysis. They state:

> Studies of religious, ethnic, political, regional and national sporting antagonisms have undergone a resurgence in the sociology of sport and, as sectarian violence – both on and off the field of play – in Northern Irish and Scottish football shows little sign of abating, a contemporary comparative analysis remains an important and significant field of enquiry.

Therefore, sports must be used to enhance cooperation and interdependencies. The comparative analysis approach is needed to effectively evaluate and understand the many psycho-social factors that dribble along with each player and team that has the ball and the imagined community of supporters cheering them on or critiquing their style of play. Sports writers will comment on the players and community approach to the game of football in a particular area. However, there is uncertainty as to whether policy makers isolate communities for the purpose of comparative analysis regarding just one sport – football. The long-term effects of social policies are generally geared toward finding the source of community problems and instituting intervention measures to eliminate their re-occurrence but often without the in-depth comparative analysis needed to arrive at workable, bipartisan solutions. Football is one of the cheapest sports to play and often becomes one of the intervention measures used for solving some community social problems. Herein lies the problem for the community and policy makers. Going to the source of the problem requires funding as well as political will. While football can satisfy some of the financial requirements, the political problems remain. The difficulty of developing this pre-requisite of a needed political will to solve certain types of social problems in the region should not be underestimated.

The politics of many states in the Caribbean does not allow for strong bipartisan debates on social issues. The adversarial nature of our political processes in the region makes consensus, even on simple issues, difficult. Developing a political will to tackle perennial social problems such as crime and violence requires more than a paradigm shift by the politicians of the various states in the region. The various elements of the political decision making matrix are all intertwined with the looming spectre of another soon-to-be-contested election, for which the politician must be prepared by assimilating all the strands of influence that lies within his/her powers. A key part of this matrix is the many different special interest groups that exert influence on the party as well as on the politician. This creates a 'black box' of binary decisions which involve satisfying these groups as well as providing good governance to the wider population. Where the two objectives coalesce, the community and nations benefit from this cosmic rarity of occurrences. Where they don't, the net result is a continuation of the status quo regarding the approach to social problem solving.

The will of the politician to solve social problems is obscured by pressure from the special interest groups, chief of which are the political party interest groups and the planter class of capitalists, sometimes neither of which sees the gain from a game of football beyond narrow political or economic interests. This latter class has the ability and resources to navigate or remain immune to social problems, even those problems created by their capitalist greed and profit imperative. The marginalised in society are not so equipped and consequently are less capable of avoiding the effect of social problems, especially those problems that remain as a cancer at the community level. The will of the politician becomes the epitome of the will of the planter class and special interest groups. Both of these groups have different objectives with regard to the solving and or complete eradication of certain social problems. The game of football as an instrument of integration has strong face validity in the community but it has its own constraints and rules while lacking the power to read the minds, perceptions and objectives of all the stakeholders involved in its execution.

How do we get the politician to make the eradication of social problems a top priority? We must begin with those groups that influence the politician. Political parties need to revisit the political education of the masses within its rank and file. They must remove the exploitative authoritarian tradition that prevents cooperative decision making and associated production efforts described by Beckford (1999). The pursuance of an integrated approach to problem solving using sports such as football as a tool is now required more than ever, given the intractable nature of current social problems. These social problems should not be seen as requiring just the attention of the current administration (whichever one is in power). The meagre resources of government and the small geographical size of our states transform these social problems into everybody's problem. The political parties, the private sector, and community groups should find common ground on how to eradicate these pressing social problems through multilateral discussions and the use of sports such as football. Prior to the discussion, it should be agreed by the politicians and all the stakeholders that decisions arrived at in these round table multilateral discussions must be binding on all the parties concerned. Bipartisan political decisions should include members of the community from all major groups. The use of sport should seek to make life better for all within the community regardless of the outcome of the various matches. This should be matched with responsible political rhetoric during and after the completion. Any plan of action must have specific time frames for implementation. Where necessary, government must be convinced to commit to providing the financing and other resources (e.g. human resources) necessary to execute the actions plans and policies.

Football and Identity

The game of football and its colonial spread is interpreted at the social level of different communities and becomes the site of intersecting trajectories of race, class, colour, politics, culture and identity. Caribbean societies are remnants of the plantation legacy of slavery. Beckford (2000) noted that contemporary Caribbean societies are continuations of the plantation society which is responsible for the legacy of social stratification and system of meritocracy that exist today in Caribbean society. The game of football is being played in contemporary Caribbean society within this same social structure which reflects the product of social stratification of race, class, colour, ethnicity and economic dependency. The functionalist Herbert Spencer contributed an organic analogy to the examination of social life. Ritzer (2008,46) opined about Spencer thus, "He was concerned about the overall structure of society, the interrelationship of the parts of society, and the functions of the parts for each other as well as for the system as a whole".

The organic approach to social enquiry can be extrapolated to understanding the sociology of football. A game of football is played at a fixed point in time with 22 players, four officials and in most cases with spectators. This setting is synchronous for the players and officials but asynchronous for some of the spectators. But, the game does not exist in isolation from the life of the community from which the players, officials and spectators are drawn. The game being played is also enmeshed with the technology, socio-politics, economic environments, values, culture and history of the country or region.

Within the process of social enquiry it is assumed that all of these forces are acting on the game at any point in time. Consequently, the effective use of the game as an intervention for the development of individuals, groups and community would involve assessment/ evaluation of all the aforementioned environmental factors. This complexity of social issues increases with the level of professionalism at which the game is played. The more teams and fans that are involved the more intense is the milieu of associated social issues. Football can be used to motivate, mobilise and guide students and residents for the development of education and the community. Football is not played within a development trajectory. For example, although Jamaica qualified for the 1998 World Cup (chapter 8) the country has been struggling to qualify since.

Issues of race, class, colour and ethnicity become intersecting sites of social construction of reality. Economic class is acknowledged as social class and race and colour are used without much reference to their etiologies. Race in Caribbean society is seen as a polysemy. There is the dominant interpretation of one's phenotypical features alongside a host of personal, communal and national interpretations that vary from area to area. The concept is so strongly embedded in the plantation society life of the region that it imbricates itself within the social and emotional psyche of the region. The game of football, at all levels, extracts strong emotional responses from all participants for various and assorted reasons.

Race is embedded in the inner logic of the Caribbean because of the history of racial oppression in the region and the nexus between skin colour and power, authority, legitimacy, status and inequality. It is not coincidental that the styles of play by some international teams from predominantly Black countries such as Brazil, Cameroon, Nigeria and Ghana have very strong support among Caribbean football fans. Games of football are not objectively watched and analysed. The racial and ethnic makeup of the teams as well as external factors such as the racial perception of the ownership of the teams and leagues play important social roles in the construction of the many perceptions surrounding the outcome and interest of the match. At the community level, the factors of race affecting a game of football may vary from the geographical position of the houses of the players in the area to the perceived colour and class of the referee. Right along the continuum from the sponsorship of the league - the largesse at stake - to the quality of playing fields, may be perceived as being racist and/or classist.

Gidden (1982) points to a distinction between class relationships emerging from the sphere of consumption and that of capitalist production. The organisers of football competitions price the entrance fees to football matches not only in relation to the profit motive but also community and spectator consumption patterns that are linked with many other social and political factors that influence the cost to enter the venues.

Class relationship characterises the dealings between governing bodies, the management of the various leagues and the players and officials. The roles of these organisations are seen as relational to the various teams which are playing the sports under their management. However, these relationships have features which can be described as hegemonic. The leadership of each governing body of football has to display an intellectual capacity that gives them legitimacy to conduct the affairs of the association or federation. Their behaviour as leaders would depict or mirror that of the ruling class in words and actions. Parkin (1982, 178) states that "Historically, the rise and consolidation of ruling groups has been effected through monopolistic control over valued resources such as land, esoteric knowledge, or arms by a limited circle of eligibles marked out by certain social characteristics." These ruling groups in the sport of football acquire control over resources which include land, buildings, fields, and sponsors' financial donations, which will then set them apart as a kind of bourgeois class. Parkins (1982, 178) further states:

> In modern capitalist society the two main exclusionary devices by which the bourgeoisie constructs and maintains itself as a class are, first, those surrounding the institutions of property; and second, academic or professional qualifications and credentials. Each represents a set of legal arrangements for restricting access to rewards and privileges: property ownership

is a form of closure designed to prevent general access to the means of production and its fruits; credentialism is a form of closure designed to control and monitor entry to key positions in the division of labour.

The bye laws and covenants of these ruling bodies of football would, as a matter of course, have these types of class relations built-in as the leaders reinforce their positions and protect themselves from the classes below. Even where broad-based support in management is required; the rules governing entry into these organisations will not be open to all and sundry but to those stipulated by the ruling monopoly.

Up until the last two decades, the sport of football in the region was very patriarchal because it was governed by men, played by men and officiated by men. The first women's World Cup was held in 1991 and several Caribbean nations now have female national football teams. Women football is growing in countries like Jamaica, Barbados, St Lucia and Trinidad and Tobago. The growth is slow because of the negative way men view the female game. While some women do not see the game as a way out of poverty and a pathway to a luxurious life, others view the game and the related opportunities differently and have taken up football scholarships in North American colleges.

The female version of the game, like so many other sports played by women, fails to attract the crowd and concomitant sponsorship that the male counterpart of the game does. The various football associations within the Caribbean and beyond would also be constrained by the many different religious beliefs about women playing sports in public. The social stratification by gender is pervasive in Caribbean football. Despite the massive globalisation of sports, women sports still lag far behind that of men. The gender problem in football is explored further in chapter 2.

Macionis and Plummer (2008, 83) note that the conflict theorists saw sports "as more obviously lined to social conflict" in society and believed that one approach by this group is "to see sports as a market involving consumerism, exploitation and opium of the masses." In applying the views of Macionis and Plummer (2008, 84) that "sports could be examined for its role in social inequalities" then one could see how the treatment of gender in football supports their view. They also share the view that' "Football belongs (at least initially) to working class men and it has a long history of being linked to macho violence and hooliganism." They however do agree that in the contemporary period football has seen a shift to the middle class with also a shift in gender. Football in the Caribbean has manifested this shift to the middle class but more in terms of management and control of the game.

Football - Lending Stability to Impoverished Caribbean Communities

Whichever Caribbean country is chosen for analysis, poverty becomes one of the pressing problems that confront policy makers. The use of football as a means of social intervention is quite popular. Many individuals look to the sport to lift them out of poverty. This happens at all levels from the schoolboy to the national team. The situation is better understood if levels of poverty in Caribbean society are examined.

The *World Bank Report* (2001) defined poverty as a pronounced deprivation in well-being and has put it in layman's terms "To be poor is to be hungry, to lack shelter and clothing, to be sick and not cared for, to be illiterate and not schooled." Poverty can be measured in two main ways.

(i) Absolute/subsistence poverty which is a state of failure to meet the bare essentials of 'physical existence'. This kind of poverty is derived through the use of a poverty line, which involves placing a monetary value on basic food items.

(ii) Relative/normative poverty. This idea identifies poverty in relation to the general standard of living and accepted quality of life.

The term poor is used as a label to indicate those individuals with limited or no access to certain goods and services considered "essential" or "basic" when compared to the rest of society.

The state of poverty in the Caribbean can also be divided into structural poverty and transitional poverty. Structural poverty affects mainly rural communities, rural women and ethnic minorities. In these communities there is a high level of illiteracy, or limited number of educated persons, individuals having little or no assets, low skills levels and little or no access to basic facilities. Whereas, transitional poverty affects persons who have little or limited access to resources but whose conditions can improve, yet they are still vulnerable to the effects of poverty.

There are numerous interrelated factors which have contributed to poverty in the Caribbean. According to *The World Bank Report* (1996) which pointed out that the factors which contribute to poverty in the Caribbean are interrelated and are; low economic growth; distortions in the labour market; and low quality social services. The sources of the region's poverty can be attributed to political, cultural, social and economic factors.

Although the countries in the Caribbean region are characterised as 'small island developing states' (SIDS), many are classed among the world's poorest. The country in the Caribbean which ranks among the poorest nations of the world is Haiti. Haiti is at the high end of the spectrum of poverty incidence with an estimated sixty five percent (65%) of its population below the poverty line.

For example, in Grenada between 30 to 40 percent of its population are living below the poverty line. *The Country Poverty Assessment* of 1998 indicated that 32.1 percent of Grenadians live below the poverty line and many of these persons had a yearly income of less than $3,300. The effect of the Great Global Recession would have resulted in an increase in the number of persons living below the poverty line due to numerous factors such as changes in the international markets, high fuel prices, impact of natural disasters, low prices on the world market for export crops, unemployment, closure of multinational firms in the manufacturing sector, fiscal difficulties resulting from high international and local debts and a negative balance of trade.

Poverty in the region, as estimated by the International Fund for Agricultural Development (IFAD) in 2002, is at 38 percent of the total population, ranging from a high of 65 percent in Haiti to a low of five percent in The Bahamas. The IFAD indicated in 2002 that almost 64 percent of the rural population in the Caribbean and Latin America live below the poverty line. The different economies of the region are vulnerable and easily affected by natural disasters, fragile democracies, as in the case of Haiti, and slow social and economic changes which have all impacted on the social problem of poverty.

According to the *Jamaica Survey of Living Conditions* (JSLC) Parish Report 2002, the parishes with the highest percentage of poor are Trelawny, Portland, St Elizabeth and Manchester. The JSLC reported that in Trelawny 31.3 percent of the persons in the parish were consuming at levels below the poverty line, significantly greater than 15.4 percent in 1992 and 18.3 percent in 1998. The same report went on to show that some 82 percent of the population in the parish of Portland had no academic qualification in 2002, some 7.4 percent had CXC general passes and 6.7 had a tertiary diploma (World Bank, 2002). Mean per capita consumption in Portland was significantly below the national levels (some 31 percent below the national mean). Moving *parri passu* with the low levels of consumption in 2002 was the poverty status of the parish which exhibited incidence of 32.3 percent of its population living in poverty, compared to the national average for Jamaica of 19.7 percent (World Bank, 2002).

Poverty is more prevalent in rural areas than in urban areas, although it may be more visible in the latter. Lack of access to physical and financial resources, production support facilities, and social and physical infrastructure services such as electricity, water, sanitation, and roads and transportation characterise rural poverty. Whereas urban poverty is revealed in overcrowding, the emergence of squatter settlements, and poor sanitation and waste disposal practices, high unemployment which results from disproportionate urban/rural migration contributes to the poverty in urban areas in the Caribbean. The issues of poverty and inequality are discussed in chapter 4 which deals with Brazil's rise as a world power and the social protests against the 2014 World Cup because of lingering poverty and inequality. The chapter ends with development lessons that the Caribbean can learn from the Brazil experience.

How can the game of football be used to solve the problem of poverty in the region? This chapter will look at some of the programmes implemented in the Caribbean to alleviate poverty. There is no magic wand of solutions to this problem of poverty. However, two factors stand out in areas of high levels of poverty; lack of adequate educational opportunities and high levels of income inequality. The use of football competitions as a stepping stone to economic freedom is quite prevalent in Jamaica. At the high school level, residential living with all meals provided becomes the norm once training starts in the summer for the upcoming academic year's football competition. The schools, sometimes with the assistance of stakeholders, past students' associations and businesses in the community are able to fund their feeding programme for the duration of the training and competition. The contribution of sports programmes to the temporary ease of poverty in many households is not documented but is an important social intervention for many families for both male and female students.

Macionis and Plummer (2008) note that the functionalist explains sports as meeting certain manifest or latent needs to make society function. The game of football is not only functional in helping to alleviate hunger and poverty in some Caribbean households, but contributes to employment and overall development. The goals of government and the private sector coalesce in providing funding for football projects that helps to uplift and develop communities through the upgrading of football fields and community centres. The private sector achieves corporate and product visibility on a regular basis. The private sector's role extends to the funding of entire programmes as named sponsors. The situation becomes a win/win for both government and the private sector with communities, groups and individuals sharing in the overall development objectives of the project.

There are many historical factors that shape the structure of these football competitions in most Caribbean countries. The system is described as sustainable development, where success is measured by the core individuals, groups and communities that benefit over a long period of time. Some of these competitions have become permanent fixtures, such as the high school leagues like Manning and DaCosta Cups in Jamaica and the Intercol in Trinidad and Tobago, and the myriad national and community leagues sustained by government, politicians, and private sector companies. Success achieved by individuals at one level is supposed to allow better access to the next level with increased social capital for the community and households. Implicit in these competitions is the assumption that an individual's success is dependent mainly on personal factors. External factors of geography, social environment, and the quality of the team, financial and other resources provided, and levels of government spending on sports are not factored into the equation to determine who moves fastest along the continuum of success. Other factors such as class, race, colour, ethnicity, and social stratification (which incorporate the aforementioned list) determine which demographic groups succeed and which ones are marginalised and headed to a life of poverty.

Inadequate use of educational opportunities and success are critical components that are sometimes far too common to some of the individuals and groups in these competitions. Some of the athletes spend long hours in training and playing at the expense of dedicating appropriate time to educating themselves. This situation is made worse by the fact that some educators tell students that only the students that are not smart should play a sport. In the end there is lack of sustainable human development for these young people who are left with very little educational qualification to show for five years or more of secondary school education. They are not able to provide for their families as a result of being unable to earn above subsistence wages. Education, adequately delivered, empowers and provides the individual with 'capabilities' to enhance their freedom that includes a living wage (Sen, 1999).

The former football players living at the minimum wage level or below becomes part of a social structure in which survival is not only his/her apogee, but also a constant struggle. This constant inability or lack of capability to do or acquire the basic things in life, results in social and psychological decisions by the individuals that are sometimes inimical to the social interest of the majority. Some of these social and psychological behaviours become social pathologies that are entrenched in the society as perennial social problems.

If the game of football in countries of the region is to help lower poverty to the point of elimination, there should be renewed efforts in policy proposals which place education within a new sociological paradigm of being part and parcel of the sports. Swift (1970) defined education as the way the individual acquires the many physical, moral and social capacities demanded of him/her by the group into which he/she is born and within which he/she must function. Swift went on to state that "the rate of social, economic and industrial change has been so great that each succeeding generation must be 'better educated' in many of the skills which are basic to the successful pursuit of occupations. Clearly parents cannot spend their own energies in providing the needed education, even if they are equipped to do it, and on the whole they cannot be. Modern society's solution is the formal system of education" (Swift, 1970, 11). This formal educational system must work in tandem with the requirement of sports to achieve the overall development of athletes while serving the objectives of the many stakeholders.

This formal system of education needs some systemic changes and new approaches if it is to help in the fight against poverty. These changes in themselves cannot be static but have the ability to respond to the ever changing requirements of the global neo-liberal economic system that created its own set of superstructures of values and beliefs. Policy makers within the region are now forced to examine the requirements of an adequate educational system which incorporates sports within the context of getting the individual to understand the wider social system and develop skills and expertise to survive.

Education is not just about providing literacy classes for those in the population who are unable to read and write. Education is designed to equip individuals with intuitive understanding of the social world around them and how to prepare and/or adjust their behaviour. The early childhood, primary and secondary phases of education are the levels at which the opportunities to inculcate this philosophy in sports, such as football, is sometime lost in the nature of Caribbean educational system. The problems that arise from the lack of a football philosophy in Jamaica are discussed in chapter 7.

The entire meritocratic system of education assumes this elusive level playing field of opportunities and capabilities. This reductionist approach to education and sports results in the marginalisation of the masses living outside of the power, privileged, and class groups who are able to achieve success in education and society. The majority of individuals living outside of this 'special group' but who have dedicated their time and bodies to playing sports such as football are faced with a matrix of possibilities for failure, where only a small percentage is able to overcome the social obstacles to success. This matrix of possibilities should become the focus of policy makers as they try to empower the masses through adequate provision of a practical educational system in which sports is given adequate recognition and funding. This will help to reduce the incidence of poverty within communities and nation states of the region. The next chapter looks at the issue of gender in football. The discrimination faced by women footballers in Jamaica means that the society is not making full use of the skills and talents of all its citizens and thus promotes the underdevelopment of communities.

Chapter 2

Hegemonic Masculinity and Women Footballers

Karen D. Madden

Introduction

In this chapter I examine the issue of gender and hegemonic masculinity through the lens of women football in Jamaica. Notions of hegemony see the dominant group, men, defining the appropriate values for the rest of the society and attempting (most times successfully) to get the society to buy into their value system. The result is that their dominance, real or imagined is maintained, which include the notions of what men and women could and should do.

Gender is socially constructed along norms and practices, so the determination of what is appropriate for men and women is encoded by societal norms. The female's physicality and her social standing are normally at the centre of notions governing what is suitable. Sport was one of the most significant avenues through which these ideas of men and their dominance were diffused. This spread included men's assertion of which games are gender-appropriate. For instance, netball is viewed as acceptable in some societies and command more media presence and sponsorship than football played by women, as football is viewed as being male appropriate. Women have competed under notions of being the "fairer" meaning weaker sex and have had to face interrogation regarding issues of stamina as well as conversations about how their biological make up will cope with the physical rigours of sports. The woman's role as the biological conduit for the birth of children as well as her place in the home to make it comfortable for the men were deemed to be her most important functions. As argued by Beckles (1995, 235) "women then are involved in a struggle to legitimise their activity within a male centre social world that sees them as competitors."

Issues of masculinity and femininity have been subjects of contested discourses in which it is posited that being masculine is akin to being powerful while being feminine is synonymous with being in subjugation. Societies in the pre-modern and the post-modern eras have rigidly imposed this power base and, by extension, determine who is powerful. "Masculinism" according to Nurse (1996) functions as a powerful ideology which has a colossal influence on how modern society is structured. In most societal strata, being masculine is represented by the dominant power base drawn along the lines of the physical superior strength of men and what manhood represents in dominating the inferior physical strength of women.

However, as women break through the glass ceiling of gender and sex, the generally held notions of masculinity and male-driven sexual identities are interrogated, resulting in contestation between the sexes. The woman participating in sport wants to be afforded the same attention and respect that her male counterpart receives. Franklyn (2009) revealed that Jamaica's track and field team to the 2008 Olympics included 28 women and 22 men, demonstrating that women are bona fide athletes. Contested roles of sexuality and what an individual perceives of herself and others' perceptions of her are intertwined discourses in formulating sexual identity and preferences. The role of the media in interrogating these inequities cannot be overemphasised. But, the media struggle with roles as defined by the corporate giants and dictated by the market or audience.

The ideology of masculine hegemony and feminine subjugation is a construction constantly contested and the subject of a magnitude of discourses. This social construction assigns roles, practice and behaviour to masculinity and similar assignments to femininity. In order to unmask the masculine hegemony that has taken a stranglehold on societies' attitudes towards women in sports, stereotypical binary notions, such as strong/weak must be removed through a process of dialogue and negotiation. There should also be an acknowledgement that notions of race, age, sexual orientation and identity and racial ethnicity intersect with gender.

Downs (2004, 107) notes that "hegemonic masculinity is a discursively constructed masculinity which gains and maintains pre-eminence through its ideological linkages with socially dominant men." When we argue about notions of hegemony, we must be careful to note that gender was not explicitly included in Gramsci's concept of hegemony. However, to the extent that media and multi-billion dollar industries that are the corporate sponsors, drive ruling class hegemony, we must concede that this powerful group guides what is covered by the media.

Notions of hegemonic dominance are maintained along lines of physical prowess, and sport in general, particularly Jamaica's football programme, reveals male dominance. When sport emerged as a way of instilling leadership skills in young men, women were excluded from active participation due to what was seen as their lack of physical strength and the perception that they were not as smart as men and did not have the capacity to be public leaders (Downer, 2004). Contestation resulted as the continued success of the woman in most societies did not result in the discontinuation of the discrimination against women. Butler (1999) notes that "woman can never be" according to this ontology of substances, precisely because they are the relation of difference, the excluded, by which that domain defines itself.

This chapter probes the notions of hegemonic masculinity to determine whether any disparities in media coverage and gender bias towards male versus female football in Jamaica is the result of this status quo. Jamaica's football is socially structured and skewed towards male domination thus receiving significantly more media coverage, sponsorship and spectator support than women's football. This attitude results in more men playing sport, more male journalists covering sport and more men are in positions of power to determine which sport gets the lion's share of sponsorship.

Gender disparities exist in the Jamaican society as it relates to the coverage of sport generally and football in particular, with media being the witting or unwitting accomplice of these notions of disparity. The question answered in this chapter is: Do the media and the public focus more on male rather than female football and why? The data for the research was collected through participant observation at a football match, a focus group interview with a group of female footballers and individual interviews with sport journalists, football coaches and a football administrator.

Sport, Gender and Hegemonic Masculinity

I use the notion of the "other" (Said, 1978) to show that hegemonic masculinity makes women the "other" because they are different from men. Hegemonic masculinity frames which sports are appropriate for women. In patriarchal Jamaica, heterosexual males form the power group and determine the values and attitudes of manhood. The issues of masculinity and femininity have been the subjects of contested discourses in which it is sometimes posited that being masculine is akin to being powerful while being feminine is synonymous with subjugation. Societies in the pre-modern and postmodern eras, have determined who is powerful and who is not and the seat of power shifts according to history and cultural relevance. In most societies, masculinity represents the dominant power base drawn along the lines of superior physical strength of man dominating the inferior physical strength of women. Women have, therefore, had to challenge a historic dichotomous "othering" of women, ergo strong/weak and the notion that men and maleness are linked to rationality and women and feminism are associated with emotionally-driven irrationality. In the interrogation of feminine and masculine roles, contestation emerges because men often feel that their manhood is under threat, and that women are seeking a reversal of the masculine hegemony masked as rights and roles. Men have been socialised to protect their manhood and strive vigorously not to be viewed as weak. The challenge that women present in attempting to assert their own importance is often seen as emasculating men. In addition, however, is the power group establishing what is manly and issues such as sexuality and strength are included in this domain. While advances have been made in how women are treated in sport, bias and prejudice still exist and these can be explained by the basis on which sport was formed. While women have become sport stars in their own right, prejudice and bias drawn along notions of gender still exist which account for how women in sport, and particularly football, are treated.

Women in sport as professionals and as amateurs form a fairly recent phenomena, and started gaining acceptance only in the twentieth century. Worldwide, women's participation in some sport is usually more acceptable than others. For instance, in the Caribbean women as netballers are more accepted than women playing football or cricket. In the United States, on the other hand, women footballers are generally accepted as in that society they are not viewed as a challenge to masculinity as American football is considered the tougher game and that is played exclusively by men. Moreover, the rights and social advancement of women have been championed by the Civil Rights Movement. The Caribbean lags behind countries like the United States in terms of the rights of citizens because the representations of femininity and masculinity in the Caribbean reveal that women are subordinated and homosexuals excluded because of the patriarchal heteronormative order in the region (Atluri, 2001).

Butler (2009) argues about the issue of gender identity by questioning, "am I that name" in which she interrogates whether the entity known as woman is only just that. To apply Butler's argument to how media managers, sponsors and even spectators view female athletes in Jamaica, it would suggest that women on the football field are viewed as women participating in sports rather than as athletes. According to Butler (2009, 6) "as a result, it becomes impossible to separate 'gender' from the political and cultural intersections in which it is invariably produced and maintained." Women in sport are affected by the male perception that they are interlopers rather than bona fide contenders.

Sage (1999) argues that gender is a factor used by media managers to shape ideology. The media select what to televise as a method of shaping ideology. One of the functions of this ideology is that female sport has been under-represented by the media in Caribbean culture. Laker (2002) note that culture is a system of shared values, meanings and symbols that enables societies and individuals to operate effectively without continually redefining these values, meanings, symbols and points of reference. Sports have meaning to participants because of the huge following it attracts, akin to religion. Important to this attraction is the duality of emotions that sports engenders, that is the pleasure and excitement of victory and the pain of defeat. Despite this duality, sport is a constant in the social milieu. Sport heroes and events are seen as legendary even though professional athletes can be viewed in the context of being workers.

Moving to other parts of the world, Matteucci (2012) revealed that gender influenced prejudices and stereotypes dominated football in Italy thereby reinforcing social distinctions and divisions. According to Cox (2004) women footballers in Australia experience misogyny and homophobia. The case of Jamaica is similar, and it is not uncommon to hear some of the players being called by unflattering names such as dike or butch (Charles, 2014a). The issue of women forcefully asserting their right to play the game of their choice was also a critical component of the fight by early female football pioneers, Nettie Honeyball and Lady Florence Dixie, in establishing the first women's league in Britain. The daughter of a working class man and the aristocrat are credited with forming the British Women's Football Club in 1894. The country was then steeped in the mores of Victorian stereotypes, women should be seen and not heard, and belonged in the home to be agents of child bearing. The notion of replacing corsets and petticoats with baggy pants and football boots was viewed as shocking by most people. The behaviour and dress of these women pushed the boundaries of political and economic correctness. Many of the female pioneer's interest in playing football was piqued by having watched the men playing and feeling that despite their smaller physical stature and the demands being placed on them to mind the children and make their men happy they should be allowed to play (Lee, 2008). These women had to overcome the social obstacles because of their gender. Similarly, chapter 5 reveals that Andrew Watson, a Black British Guianese and one of the world's greatest footballers also had to overcome prejudices during this period because of his race.

The historical context of the day was perhaps the biggest challenge the women faced. Victorian mores and ideas meant that women did not leave home without their menfolk and their clothing marked their places as women. Women who were "allowed" to play sports such as hockey and bicycling did so wearing the long skirts and corsets of the day. The lady footballers of Britain were adamant that they wanted to wear clothing appropriate for the game of football and did not see it as some pastime, they were serious footballers. Therefore, when they pushed back against the stereotype and donned the gear worn by men they were not just getting dressed in appropriate wear for the game, they were making a political statement and championing a fundamental right for women, their right to choose (Lee, 2008).

The Struggle of Jamaican Women Footballers

The World Cup is the symbol of football supremacy which is played every four years by several of the biggest football nations in the world. Jamaica's football programme is epitomised by the world renowned Reggae Boys, the nomenclature for the national senior football men's team. The nation's highest achievement was reaching the finals of the 1998 World Cup in France. Football remains the country's most popular sport and is played across all demographics and at all levels, from primary school to university and club teams and private sector teams (The Business House Competition). Several of the nation's top male footballers have been able to secure a considerable income by playing in the top leagues around the globe, including the English Premier League. This results in a domino effect with thousands of footballers seeking to make a name in this very lucrative market since the players earn millions in salaries as well as endorsement deals.

The Kingston and St Andrew Football Association (KASAFA), the governing body for football in the Kingston Metropolitan Region, credits Jamaican Jean Elaine Nelson as being largely responsible for Jamaica's first organised women's league in 1989. According to the KASAFA website, the Jamaican league began in response to the need for Jamaica to field a women's team for the first World Cup for women. "The talk in the air was 'time was running out for Jamaica' and the country would miss the boat to China as that country was awarded host nation of FIFA's first Women's World Cup in 1992. The fever had caught on all over the world and there was an explosion of female interest in football. It dawned on the then 31-year-old Mutual Security Bank clerk that 'nutten a gwaan a yard,'(nothing is happening at home) and, further, Jamaica had nothing in place for CONCACAF Women's Qualifying Tournament scheduled for Haiti in April 1991. As far as Jean Nelson was concerned, there was no formal competition and constitutional structure in place for Jamaican women to play a leading role and mobilise a national team to respond to the challenge of the two historic football events." Prior to Nelson's epiphany, earlier efforts by Andrea Lewis of Boys Town Wild Cat, Concorde's Bernadatte Mairs and the Boogie Girls' Karlene Bonner, at organising a women's league were thwarted, largely due to the prejudices against women at the time. Nelson buoyed by the potential of Jamaica playing in the qualifying competition and the possibility of playing in the Women's World Cup presented a new fight for women to be organised for action (KASAFA, 2014).

The inaugural women's competition kicked off on Saturday, January 20, 1990 with four teams, Priory, Mico, Boogie Girls and Boys' Town Wild Cats. The Jamaica Women's Football Association (JWFA) was formed months later on May 10, 1990. Jean Nelson was elected president with Karlene Bonner, Vice-President; Janet Martin, secretary; Jean Cover, treasurer; Grace Butterfield, assistant secretary while Andrea Lewis was co-opted as technical adviser. KASAFA's website quotes Nelson in her presidential address to the JWFA's first Congress on May 10, 1990:

> To establish women's football in Jamaica, we know we have first to overcome these historical myths and sexual bias that mitigate against our ladies being involved in this male sport. We need your understanding and support to overcome this barrier and to bring our talented sportswomen into this 20th century sport which has already created female soccer stars in the developed countries.

The league took "baby steps" and only focused on a corporate area league, but in 1995 the JWFA assumed full responsibility as more rural teams expressed an interest in participating in the league. In keeping with FIFA rules, the JWFA was eventually disbanded and the responsibilities for women's football fell under the aegis of the JFF with a sub-committee administering the work of the women's league.

Women's football has been growing in popularity globally. The increased number of women participating in what is considered male-dominated sport is in tandem with the increased pressure on the so-called glass ceiling by women and the increased claims women are making in social and economic spheres. Since its formalisation in 1990 Jamaica has managed to assemble a good squad which has performed creditably in the region even though so far they have failed to qualify for the Women's World Cup. Some of the players have been able to secure scholarships to colleges locally and overseas. It should be noted here that the JFF, the governing body for football in Jamaica, subsequently suspended the women's senior programme because of a lack of funds. However, the nation operates a national premier league, and while the women do not attract the level of support in sponsorship and spectator base, the sport has been growing in popularity as the skill set of the players improve. The national women's football programme was restarted in 2014.

The Barbican versus Portmore Game at the End of Round Final 2012
This section outlines the information gathered from the participant observation at a football game and a discussion of the data and sets the background for the remainder of the chapter. The observed game pitted defending champions of the women's National Premier League (NPL) Barbican Women's Football Club up against the second place finishers Portmore Women's Football Club in an end of round championship decider game. The game was played at the Spanish Town Prison Oval in St Catherine. The afternoon encounter saw a fairly large spectator support representing the popularity of the nation's two top women's football teams. The spectators were males and females, mostly young people between the ages of 18 and 30, with a smattering of older folks and children. Media support was sparse with only two television cameras and one print journalist present. The President of the Jamaica Football Federation was noticeably absent (himself or his representative always attend a male championship game) and no announcement was made as to whether he had tendered apologies or whether anyone was representing him, given that the women's league falls under the auspices of the JFF. The highest ranking football officer at the game was the President of the St Catherine Football Association, since the finals were being held in St Catherine.

The football fans at the game displayed a wealth of knowledge of the game and some of them seemed very familiar with the players on the field. Some of the players had come out of the high schoolgirls' league and had been playing in the club system for several years, with a few having played in the national programme. It was evident that there were a number of fans in the modest venue and they showed rowdy support for their team. Noticeably, a number of women present wore traditional male style dress, boot cut jeans, shirts or polo shirts, boots or slippers. Several of these women appeared to have attended the game as lesbian couples. They appeared to be at home in the crowd, sat with each other and from time to time shared whispers and affectionate laughter with each other.

Among the spectators young men could be heard loudly questioning the sexuality or sexual orientation of the women on the field as well as those in the stands. "Da gyal deh look like a man star" (That girl looks like a man), "no dawg a man dat, a mus lesbian, dem gyal yah deh wid one anoda. Dem must be lesbian" (No dog, she is a man. These girls are seeing each other. They are lesbians). Even the players on the field who appeared to be above average in their football competence were likened to men. "Yow Jah know da gyal deh kick di ball like a man" (Hey, God knows that girl kicks the ball like a man) and "She dribble like a man star." Interestingly, when spectators occasionally yelled to their favourite player "man on" to indicate that they were facing an incoming tackle from an opponent, one of the women in the stands would retort "no, you mean woman on" to riotous laughter from the others in the group. It should be pointed out, however, that the term "man on" is a widely used football slang and it did not appear that the fans who used it meant to be discriminating. However, what this term demonstrates is the male-dominated history of the game to the point that it has developed male specific terminologies.

Verbal attacks on referees are very much the norm at football matches in Jamaica. Generally, when the referee makes a call which earns the wrath of a spectator verbal abuse would be hurled his way with suggestions about actions he can take with his mother, or the prime minister or the JFF president or a club president, in fact any notable person in the society. In this case, the all-woman referee squad was not spared verbal abuse, in fact the abuse appeared to be far in excess of what the male referees usually had to contend with.

However, they were spared the missiles being hurled on the field. Men yelled that she should "suck har modda" (suck her mother's vagina) or "suck har man hood" (suck her boyfriend's penis). Ironically, in one case a woman who dressed like a man, yelled to the referee "hey referee gyal yu ah si yu period" (Hey referee girl are you menstruating?). This reference to the monthly menstrual cycle of women was significant.

Discussion of the Participant Observation

Since Victorian times, and as manifested by the comment above about the menstrual cycle, women have been considered to be irrational, emotional and even mentally sick during their monthly menstrual period. Being a referee, the arbiter of the game requires a sound mind, quick thinking, emotional stability and intimate knowledge of the rules of the game which must be decided on quickly and firmly. It appeared from this comment that this woman had bought into the gender ideology that women "at their time of month" could not make important decisions as required of a referee. The fact that it was a woman and one who resembled a man, speaks to the extent that women have also accepted the world view of dominant males.

The verbal attacks on the players and the referees were the result of the thinking that the women were encroaching on what was considered male-dominated territory. Women were challenging the established hegemony of the masculine stereotype associated with football and therefore had to be put in their places by an onslaught of verbal abuse. Football was meant to be male territory, controlled by the boys, free from the girls and featuring crotch grabbing and misogynistic comments.

The women's game has grown exponentially in Jamaica because of wider social acceptance, the audacious stance of the women and their developing skills. The women players sought to challenge this stereotype of women's frailty by appearing manly and strong and wearing androgynous clothing. The lack of media presence at the end of round final was not surprising, given the sparse support from the media at other women's games that I had attended. Media drives attitudes and therefore for any cultural phenomenon or event to be successful it must have "buy in" from the media. Today's women play under the shadow of having to convince the society, in general, that they have the physical ability and knowledge to play the game and were also fighting against the stereotype of being lesbians/gays/butch because they were playing a sport the society deems a man's game.

The attitudes of the contemporary Jamaican spectators are similar to that of the spectators in the nineteenth century game in Britain. While there was the dominant theme that women should not be playing football because it was a man's game, a woman who showed good footballing skills would receive grudging respect. However, that respect would be framed within issues of sexuality and gender. She was either gay or a man disguised as a woman. In the Victorian era it could be assessed as a reluctance to accept change and in the present era it can be read as misogyny. Women playing football bucked established stereotypes and the historical base of Victorian standards and decorum for women was a contentious time for the game to have developed. The reality of a society steeped in Victorian norms from which two women from different strata emerged to form a women's league of a men's game was salient irony. The evolution of women's dress from corsets and petticoats and flowing skirts to baggy pants to the situation today where women on the football field wear the same clothing as their male counterpart traces the development of the game and evaluation of attitudes and how women have been able to make strides despite the prejudices then and now.

However, despite these strides women's physical build continue to offer challenges on the field of play. In the game when one player skilfully controlled a powerfully placed ball on her chest, the reaction of a male spectator was "she nuh wah dem breast deh" (She doesn't want her breasts) which he repeated three times to ensure maximum reach to all spectators close to him. Similar plays witnessed in the men's game were greeted by approving shouts of "ball" meaning that was an excellent control of the ball.

In contemporary football, the women who look feminine are assumed to be mediocre players or are subject to cat calls and wolf whistles from the men while the women who are sturdier looking coupled with good ball handling skills are assumed to be lesbians. Women who cannot play are seen as representing their gender and receive blanket treatment "that's why woman nuh fi play football" (That's why women should not play football). A woman who can play is representative of herself but is viewed as a man, "dah gyal deh play like man een star" (That girl plays like a man). The women's game is framed by the notion that football was manly and only men could keep it well and truly masculine, while women should know their place. The spectators in the Victorian era, as do contemporary spectators, dealt with gender confusion where women are viewed as abdicating their role and responsibility as women to become "men" on the football field. In the days of the Lady Footballers in Britain at least two players with considerable skills, were nicknamed "Tommy" by the spectators. They insisted in fact that the players could not be girls. Lee (2008) described one as a girl between 11 and 13 years of age, but the spectators insisted that the player was a boy based on the skills she displayed.

Today there are several players in the Women's Premier League as well as the school girl's league in Jamaica who are nicknamed with male monikers and it is not uncommon to hear the fans hail "Messi," "Makerel," "Bailey," "String bean," and "Piggy" as they cheer for their team. Invariably it is the sexuality of the players who resemble men that is questioned and not those who look softer or more feminine. In fact, a spectator remarked that one player "too pretty fi play football" (too pretty to be playing football). Discussions regarding the journey of women's football would be skewed if it was not pointed out that the game in developed countries is well respected and the players are considered celebrities. Female football is accepted in these societies. The United States Women's Football Team won the first women's World Cup in 1991 and the game has attracted international and domestic attention. Performance has been rewarded with acceptance. This team has won several other major championships and Olympic medals. This, of course, is a cultural phenomenon since football (or soccer as the Americans refer to it) is not a comparatively popular game in the United States, which boasts its own version of football, which is more akin to rugby.

The attitude towards sexuality was famously brought to the fore after the US women's team won the 1999 World Cup and Brandi Chastain after scoring the winning goal whipped off her shirt revealing her sports bra. That picture was later published in *Sports Illustrated* as well as several newspapers worldwide, including *Time* and *Newsweek*. Men footballers take their shirts off on many occasions after scoring and most times are rewarded with a caution card from the referee. That a woman had revealed her femininity and sexual appeal was the only reason that picture became so famous.

The women's game in Jamaica has not been able to pull in the spectators in the way the American counterpart has. However, the Jamaican team has some good players, many of whom play for the country's top clubs and have landed scholarships to pursue degrees in overseas universities. We should encourage and support more young women to pursue this path. Another factor which must be considered in framing the women's football situation in Jamaica and the attitudes towards the game is the country's economic base. The focus of the JFF is the men's programme. The JFF has consistently complained that it is short of funds to run the various programmes and has sought to pressure the government into giving it access to more funds.

Interviews with Journalists, a Coach and an Administrator

Female football administrator who works with men's and women's teams

The NPL for men is played over a nine month period, as opposed to the women's, which lasts about four months. The media is therefore able to provide longer coverage. There is also extensive coverage of Super League Confederation titles which will confirm the teams vying for a place in the NPL. Therefore, the progress of teams is tracked from an early stage. The Women do not have such a league at the parish level which would provide for constant coverage and excitement into their NPL season.

There is a disparity in the standard of play in men and women games, due to the following reasons: most parish associations have mandatory competitions for boys, that is, the under 13, under 15, under 17, and the under 20 age groups. As such, boys are playing football for a longer period of time. Most girls do not start playing organised football until they reach high school. At that time, most coaches focus on winning, as opposed to teaching the technical aspect of the game, thus making the game unattractive to watch from a purist point of view, and not providing value for money from a sponsor's point of view.

Women's football in Jamaica has not been marketed as attractive, as the media tend to focus on the negatives; such as the way the girls act and dress. The fact is that a number of girls during the last 10 years (approximately 60 that have played in the Premier League) have received football scholarships, both locally and abroad. The low level of media coverage is based on the low importance the stakeholders place on the product (women's football). Sponsors are not necessarily made aware of the social impact of assisting and contributing to women's football. The media is not willing to take a chance on women's football by even having delayed coverage of local games.

The exposure would give potential sponsors an opportunity to see the possible value of their support. Coverage would possibly show little girls that they can play football, which would widen the base of girls that the clubs and national programme would have to choose from. So the media has a major role to play in assisting to break down the barriers that do exist, when it comes to both coverage and support from potential sponsors and the public.

A women's football coach

There is definitely more focus on the NPL for men because this is the top league in Jamaica and as such is more marketable to sponsors and fans. The women's NPL is fairly new and is struggling for acceptance from some football administrators and, more so, sponsors. There is a disparity between the quality of men's and women's competitions, but put in proper perspective the competitive nature of play in both leagues are almost at the same intensity. There is a definite bias against the women's game; from media coverage to sponsors. The reality is, if the women's NPL had more exposure in the media, the interest from sponsors would be increased. As it stands now there is no coverage, except for the odd report in the sports news. The fan base is mostly made up of past players and not people from communities as obtains in the NPL for men. Women's football is frowned upon by most males in the media, and companies do not see it as a viable investment, even before giving it a chance. Most males are still of the impression that women should not be playing football.

Sports journalist 1

Based on history and tradition, there has been more focus by the media on the men's premier league than the women's. There has been a structured senior level men's football competition from in the 1950s coming up to when it was re-branded the NPL in 1983. The Tivoli Gardens team won the championship that year. There has been a natural attraction to the men's NPL for journalists, station administrators and sponsors and this will be the case for a very long time. No doubt, the women's premier league has been growing in recent years and thanks to sponsors like Sherwin Williams, and before that Captain's Bakery, who have invested heavily in women's football hence it has definitely received more visibility while the administrators of local football have taken it under their wings hence we are seeing more publicity in the media. The FIFA President did say a few years ago that women's football is the future of the sport, so based on his calculations this may very well be the case in Jamaica. However, for it to begin to make inroads into the men's game women's football might have to begin to make a fashion statement on the field to attract men to matches. But, for now, because it has been deeply grounded in our society, our journalists, media managers and sponsors will be more into the men's game because of the faster and more physical nature of the beautiful game.

Sports journalist 2

The men's NPL gets far more coverage than the women's by the media. The male dominated sports get more sponsorship and sponsors tend to brand the sport and with this they get the necessary publicity. Women's football is improving. However, they do not get the same coverage. Some journalists follow the league but not with the intensity they give the men's game. The national team reaching the World Cup and some club teams playing in the Caribbean /CONCACAF competition has helped the men. Although the women have gone on for World Cup qualification the same level of coverage is not evident. The media follow men far more than they follow the women. The quality of play from the men is higher than that of the women. However, the women have been improving with the schoolgirl league which attracts a lot of supporters but still does not see any media support. There have been some very good and competitive intercollegiate female games without coverage. This can be a case of lack of knowledge. It is unfortunate that gender is an issue in how sport is treated and the level of disparities. We have very few female managers, coaches and sports journalists. Look at our female team coached by men and even in netball at the club level and now some of the national coaches are men.

Sports journalist 3

There is clearly more focus by the media on coverage of the NPL for men in comparison to the female competition. I don't get the feeling that there is yet a wide acceptance of women playing the game or women's ability to entertain while playing the game and so is depicted through sponsorship support and media coverage. One must point out, though, that while this has improved over time it is nowhere near the level of men. I think there is a disparity in the quality of men's football versus the quality of women's football. I feel the quality of women's football has improved, however it still is not at the level that would send the normal man frenzied thinking about it. I also feel this is behind the attitude of media and even administrators. For example, when the JFF was in financial crisis two years ago the senior female programme was the one that got cut. I think, generally, men are thought to be superior to women in any sport and is not an issue that is unique to football. So, maybe there are preconceptions as it relates to what women can do on a football field. These preconceptions must affect the way sponsors, media and even administrators think.

Sports journalist 4

As a matter of fact major media in Jamaica in particular and the world in general tends to focus more on men's football than women's football without any vindictive or sexist motive. I really can't understand this compulsion to make this like so many other issues, a "gender issue." It's very simple, men's football is bigger than women's football locally and internationally. Men's football is a bigger spectacle which generates bigger business, and from the perspective of the media it is bigger news. It is as simple as that. There is a disparity in the quality of men's football compared to women's football. That is totally understandable. Men's football is more than two centuries old. Women's football is a relatively new activity. How realistic is it to expect the women's game to all of a sudden catch up and be equal to the men's game in terms of popularity, appeal, and ultimately media coverage? Again, as far as football is concerned I don't see any gender discrimination. The disparity in coverage, sponsorship, and general public interest and so on, all comes down to the superior appeal of the men's game over the women's game.

A sports editor

From an editor's point of view, I always stress the coverage of men's and women's events with an even hand. In other words, what I decide to cover and instruct the staff to cover, follow the basic principles of journalism rather than, is it male or female? I make my decision based on how important the event is, the stage where it is and the available resources I have. So from a personal standpoint, I never see male and female events, but sporting events and try to be fair and equal in the coverage. I might not always succeed, because the reporters might do something else, whether justified or not. I think it would be good to speak to individual reporters privately on these issues. My own concern is that I have never thought about live radio coverage of the women's NPL. The inadequate media coverage women's sport receives is more a tradition than an approach. I try to take women's football to a level but this depends on the availability of resources and staff.

I think the disparity in the quality between men's and women's football is an important factor. We tend to go for high quality and fast-paced excitement in the products we cover, especially live on radio, even less so on television. However, the female football specifically is "purer" than the men's soccer, meaning that the girls are all about the game and are less distracted by side issues. I also see that women are less distracted in World Cup finals.

For sports coverage, the issues of disparities in gender issues do not arise. We do not see gender or any other issues, other than can I get to this event, and if the resources are available we will get it done. This approach is no different than how we approach a male event.

Discussion of the Individual Interviews

The dominant theme in these individual interviews was the disparity in the coverage of men and women's football. Various opinions were offered to explain this disparity but the thoughts are coded along gender differences and attitudes towards those differences. The history of both games is a factor which affects this attitude. Women's football is a very new cultural phenomenon compared with the men's game. In Jamaica the history is even shorter. The standard of play among women also impacted on how seriously the purists of the game take this version. The coaches agree that women learn football skills later in life than men. Most little boys are kicking a box at a very tender age which hones their skill and appreciation of the game. Girls are generally not allowed to partake in what parents consider to be this "boyish" game. Therefore, when a girl finally decides to play football competitively she has to be taught the fundamentals of the game. However, this is lost on some coaches resulting in some women being weaker in some of the fundamentals of being a good footballer. The respondents also cited the overt focus on sexuality by some spectators, even some with a very high appreciation for football. This overt focus on the players' sexuality results in major distractions from the game to instead focus on interrogating the women's sexuality. By extension sponsors are seemingly not drawn in large numbers to the game due to the unattractiveness of women dressed like men and the assumptions about the women's sexuality. The interview respondents pointed to a clear gender disparity with women's football not being given live coverage whereas men's football is routinely carried live. This exists at the school level as well as at the level of the NPL.

At the schoolboy level the Manning Cup, DaCosta Cup, Olivier Shield, Ben Francis Cup and Walker Cup are named competitions which are symbols of male football supremacy among high schools in urban and rural Jamaica. In the case of the Olivier Shield this is played between the winners of the urban Manning Cup and the rural DaCosta Cup competitions. Competitions between the schools are fierce and adults who have long graduated from school attend the packed games. Selected games are shown live on local television and broadcast on radio stations while the semi-finals and finals of all the championships are carried live. The media also provide bio data on the players and background information and vital statistics of the schools. On the contrary, the high schoolgirl football competition has one cup played among a significantly smaller number of schools and not even the final game is broadcast live. At least one sports editor insisted that this disparity in coverage is not due to any premeditated decision at his level. It should also be pointed out that the high school boys' football competition has been played for several decades, much longer than the school girl competition and has the backing of a formidable slate of private sector sponsors.

One positive pointed out by the interview respondents is that women mostly concentrate on the purity of the game rather than the other side issues, such as ego that often accompanies the male game. This difference could be attributed to the notion that women are often more focused than men, and that they are usually less affected by their egos. Competing masculinities usually result in fierce contestation on the field of play. There are men who are built with larger physical frames, there are men who are from affluent backgrounds, fair skinned, wearing fancier gear with the dichotomy being men from the poor inner city that are dark skinned and have less disposable income. The differences in socioeconomic background and values often result in conflicts. Some of the conflicts on the field of play have nothing to do with football.

The failure of the media to highlight more of the games played by the women results in a lack of public attention and sponsorship support. Sponsors seldom support an unknown product. Perhaps, if the sponsors were to be persuaded by the administrators of women's football to support the product, that would propel the media to highlight the games that translate to more public support and a change in attitudes towards the women and their game. However, some of the interview respondents point to the relative newness of the women's game and believe this is at the heart of the reticence to accept it as another cultural expression.

Another point highlighted here, and which was a theme in discussions with other groups, was the absence of overt sex appeal (meaning heterosexual appeal) in the games. Sponsors like an attractive product and sex sells. Therefore, it is felt that if the women playing football were sexier or highlighted their sexiness, similar to women in tennis or netball, then more support would come their way. Some of the journalists pointed to the women wearing sexy apparel and showing more of their physique, and pushing their womanliness as a way of bringing more attention and a greater acceptance of their game. This change of dress would reduce the feeling among men and some women that only "dykes" play women's football.

Focus Group Discussion with Women Footballers

The focus group was a women's football team of 15 players of one of the teams in the NPL for women. The players ranged in ages from 17 to 25 and some were university and high school students while others were working in various jobs. All agreed to share their views about women in football.

The players are of the belief that women's football suffered bias and posited that this bias was gender based. According to them, more attention was paid to men's football than to women's football from the citizenry and from the media. They argued that perceptions of their ability as women to play as well as or better than men was at the heart of the disparities. In addition, the stereotype that women who play football are lesbians was also a factor for the negative reaction. But the players also blamed some of their peers for this negative stereotype. They pointed to female players who dressed and acted like men. The presence of lesbians on some teams, they felt, was not so much a problem as women who acted and dressed like men. The female players also pointed to the bias faced by male netballers and felt culture and society were responsible for this. They cited the United States' women's football programme which they noted was equal to English Premier League. The players pointed to the politics of play on the field and felt that men would not allow women to outperform them. This stance was based on the notion that men were supposed to rule, they were the breadwinners, while women belonged in the household. Some women dressed and acted like men and even told their female opponents "I'm a man, don't tackle me." The players noted that even in their families and among their friends there was concern about their sexuality and the view that football was not an appropriate sport for women. In addition, some women thought that they had to project a masculine look in order to be taken seriously as a footballer.

These women believed that if they "look girly" the assumption would be made that they were not good footballers and to contest that notion, some women footballers dressed like men and adopted a male stance. The women in the focus group felt, however, that these women should take their place on the football field and allow their performance to speak for them. The challenge here they noted, though, is that women have to work harder to prove themselves as competent and serious players. One of the factors the players felt that resulted in minimal private sector sponsorship for the women's programme, is that the sponsors are turned off by the presence of too many male-looking players and prefer better representation of their products on and off the field. The players feel women are judged more harshly when they display acts of indiscipline. "Women have to be disciplined because when a woman gets angry on the football field it is ugly." The players believed that society tolerates acts of indiscipline, such as temper tantrums, rough tackle and fights, from men at a higher level than it does of women. The group also felt that on the field one should be viewed as a footballer, not as a man or a woman. It's difficult or next to impossible for a sponsor to attach their brand to a product that is seen to represent values that they know the majority of Jamaicans have a problem with, such as homosexuality.

The female players' perception of the disparity of attitudes and media coverage is that this is along gender lines. While acknowledging that the quality or standard of their play was sometimes at a lower level than the men, they argued that this did not affect the level of competition in the women's league and believed that it was more perception than reality that was preventing their game from being attractive to sponsors and by extension the media.

The women argued that stereotypical generalisations such as one that assumes that all women who play football are lesbians as well as the presence of several women who dressed like men was to be blamed for negative reactions to the game. The bias is further exacerbated by the open acknowledgement that some of the women are in fact lesbian and teammates are sometimes lovers. Lovers' spats have been known to disrupt training and at least one coach shared that he has had to intervene in tension involving former lovers. Women players are treated as the other having to validate their right to play, balancing that with how to attract media and sponsorship support.

Discussion of the Focus Group Interview

The focus group respondents revealed that men with the ideology of hegemonic masculinity policed the "male and female sports" for deviations from expected gender roles and the sexuality of people. Deviations from the expected gender role have social consequences. These women experience verbal attacks and ridicule on the field of play and on the streets because they push against the norms and values of hegemonic masculinity. Women who play football are deemed to be men so much so that "soft women" do not have the skills to play the game because they play like women. Therefore, some women in response to the attacks against the soft women dress and play aggressively like men so they will be respected for their footballing skills.

Some of the women that dress like men and play football aggressively are, in fact, lesbians. However, they and others are called lesbians not because they publicise their sexuality but because normal women do not play football, a man's sport. Therefore, women who play football must be the abnormal lesbians. These women find that they become the abnormal "other" of the men who espouse traditional gender roles and police the sexuality of other citizens. They are not alone in the "othering" they experience because men who play netball are deemed to be gay men because they are playing a woman's sport.

The media is accused of not giving adequate coverage to female football games not just because the women are not taken seriously but also because many journalists believe that many of the women who play football are lesbians. These women believe that journalists are some of their oppressors. The reports of discrimination of stigmatised and oppressed groups should be taken seriously. This finding about the female footballer's perception of the media in this chapter is corroborated in the study conducted by Charles (2014a) which found that the women footballers argued that the media was biased in their coverage of women footballers.

The women noted that they are judged more harshly than men because they are women and the range of negative stereotypes that are used to frame their participation in sports. There was an irony indicative of stigmatised groups in that some of the women didn't only blame the critics of women playing football but also female footballers that dressed like men. These women who dressed like men were partly responsible for how female footballers were portrayed.

Conclusion

The research discussed in this chapter reveals that there is more and differential media coverage of male football competitions compared to female football competitions. The journalists argue that this is so because female football attracts little or no sponsorship. There is also the perception among many people that the skill set of Jamaican female footballers is less than that of male footballers such as how they pass the ball, read or interpret the game, throw in a ball and so on. The spectators feel that women should not be playing football because it is a man's game. Since football is a man's game female footballers must be lesbians. Moreover, football is a dangerous game for women. Football is a dangerous game for all if the sport which is popular in the inner city is not used to enhance community development in these poverty stricken areas. The next chapter discusses the role of football in community development in Greater August Town.

Chapter 3

Football, Culture and Community Development in Greater August Town

Olivene Burke, Tarik Weekes and Wanda M. Costen

Introduction

Jamaica is a country of approximately 2.7 million people, making it one of the largest English-speaking nations in the Caribbean. For more than a decade, the country has struggled with economic and social development issues such as enclave development and poverty, negatively impacting on the ability of several Jamaicans to experience any enhancement in the material condition of their lives. Despite the wide-reaching local and internationally-supported economic stabilisation and adjustment programmes, implemented to change the economic environment of the nation, there has not been a significant advancement in production indicators suggestive of that desired change.

The research on the relationship between culture and the playing of football in Greater August Town (GAT) was prompted by the need to understand what assets the people and the community had that could be maximised for the shaping and realising of community development. The authors are in no way suggesting that the derivatives from playing football be taken as a panacea for breaking down barriers to community development. Instead, playing football should be seen as one of the means to fostering social integration, inclusion and participation of people which are requirements for development. As this chapter highlights, the playing of football in GAT has the potential of contributing to community development. The research is qualitative so the goal is to identify if playing football is linked to the identity of the people in GAT and, if so, is there any sporting capital that can be used for the overall benefit of the community. Sporting capital can be described as attitudes and attributes in individuals and groups of persons that are part of their normative behaviour while engaged in sports and which can contribute to the improvement of their lives. Rowe and Norden (2013, 1) describe sporting capital as:

> Analogous to the theory of human capital and can be defined as the stock of physical, social, psychological attributes and competencies that support and motivate an individual to participate in a sport and to sustain that participation over time.

At a more macro level, it has as much to do with resources in the community that can go hand-in-hand to assist with the maximisation of these individualistic associations with attributes of sporting behaviour. Sporting capital is not to be confused with the other forms of capital cited by Pierre Bourdieu. Skinner, Zakus and Cowell (2008, 256) citing Bourdieu (1986) note his recognition of economic capital, social capital and cultural capital. They explain:

> Economic capital is linked closely with and convertible to money and institutionalised into forms of property rights. Cultural capital on the other hand is often institutionalised in the form of educational qualifications and school ties while social capital is related to the social connections people have developed or maintain.

An exploration of the spread of acceptance and depth of playing football in GAT can help with the construction of solutions to be incorporated in community development work in GAT and other communities.

Background on Greater August Town

Greater August Town is one of several communities located in eastern St Andrew, Jamaica. As of 2013, it was home to approximately 16,000 residents. Five districts make up GAT: August Town, Bedward Gardens, African Gardens, Hermitage and Goldsmith Villa. The community is characterised by very hilly terrain in some parts, a river which divides Bedward Gardens from the other four districts and what appears to be an abandoned quarry in the north eastern part of the community.

Between 1980 and 2005, the community was plagued by collective violence spurred by partisan politics and the desire to control political turf to gain more votes. One resident, who was interviewed in the research that informs the ideas of this chapter, recalled the early 1970s when the community was peaceful and people moved about freely and getting people involved in empowering activities was his concern and that of many others. By the early 1980s the atmosphere had changed and sporting activities which brought the community closer were discontinued. This experience was repeated in the mid-1990s and between the years 1999 and 2005, it was clear that the way of life of the people who lived in GAT was largely being affected by short and long intense periods of collective violence. The interpersonal and collective forms of violence that were featured divided individuals from personal and organisational standpoints. On the personal level, residents who were interviewed spoke of not being able to cross borders which prevented their interaction with friends and family who had settled in other districts of the community. However, the fear of interaction with others because of location did not threaten public participation in sporting and entertainment activities. All individuals interviewed in the community-wide data collection process highlighted the integration that took place on days such as Emancipation Day, which was a cultural day in the community that featured road races and matches across various activities and sports.

Greater August Town is a resilient community. While there have been severe bouts of violence and crime, this anti-social behaviour is not representative of all the people and districts in GAT. For the last ten years law enforcement has experienced difficulty with one particular corner in the community which has behaved anti-socially to other corners and districts in the community in its quest for turf. Even then, this is not representative of the behaviour of all residents living in that corner. In 2008, a peace agreement with support from the police, community based organisations, the Peace Management Initiative and the UWI was signed by warring gangs in the community. Since the signing a gradual reduction in murders and shootings has been experienced in the community. According to the Jamaica Constabulary Force there were four murders in the

75

community in 2011. Unfortunately, murders rose to 11 in 2012 but decreased significantly, to six in 2013.

There are many different community based organisations (CBOs) in GAT working towards the improvement in the lives of residents. The promotion of non-violence, creating a safe community and developing individuals are targeted at vulnerable groups such as the youth, women and fathers. In May 2013, a workshop conducted in leadership for representatives of CBOs revealed that there were at least 20 different CBOs in GAT.

Conceptualisation of Key terms

Culture is defined as the way of life of a people. It has to do with the experience of people and their connectedness to others. This connectedness that people feel with each other provides a sense of belonging and defines how they behave with each other and over time is the consensus of accepted practices of behaviour. Culture is very complex and becomes harder to define when we examine its features across various groups of people. Thus you can experience various cultures within a universally-recognised culture. The various cultures can be based on differences people have emerging from their ethnicity, shared histories and even class. Culture can be material and non-material or a social, economic or political force. Giroux (2000) says that culture is central to the understanding of struggles over meaning, identity and power. Chai (2011, 1033) posits that despite the many definitions of culture, all of them share the idea that culture is a collective phenomenon applied to a particular group or society, whether it describes "consensually held attitudes, a distribution of such attitudes or an emergent entity that cannot be described as an aggregation of individual attitudes."

The playing of football, which has cultural connotations, is an action that can be engaged by people of both sexes at a recreational, grassroots or professional level. As with other sporting disciplines, the playing of football can be interpreted as having some form of meaning and not just serving a function. There is no straightforward explanation for the term playing football, but from several observations and insights from the literature, it can be deduced that

76

it is an outdoor activity happening within no specific geographic space, except where it is being played professionally and played on a field. It also has various participants. Some participants are central to the playing of the game and others are not. The more central include the players, coaches and or a manager, a manager's assistant, someone in charge of inventory and supplies, sponsors or financiers and fans. The inclusion of the latter is particularly important, because of the growth of fandom. Heavy commercialisation and consumption have become synonymous with the products associated with the playing of football. These core fans are important to the reproduction of the football spirit which involves ritualistic practices accompanied by language, dress, integration and exclusiveness.

Community development is about people and what they do to help each other (Vail, 2007; Spruill, Kenney& Kaplan, 2001). It has roots in various disciplines and has been explained in different ways by different writers and interpreted to mean different things to different people in different places. Vail (2007, 572) argues that "the fundamental element of all community development initiatives is about people helping improve their life conditions by addressing common interests". Therefore, community development is a change process which may be facilitated by other people, but is community determined. Skinner, Zakus and Cowell (2008) see community development as bolstering community processes and social resources through the creation of consensus, activities and social networks outside the family that residents say will enhance their area as a better social space in which to reside and work.

Theoretical Underpinnings

The playing of football presents an interesting perplexity about human behaviour and institutions that are involved. It is a structured game that can happen across various social and cultural contexts, it has its own rules, power brokers and power wielders but within that system is the opportunity to exercise actions and decision making based upon a role that has been preconceived for an individual. Players exercise agency but, much like how the body as a living organism functions, they do so within a particular role that must be fulfilled for the greater good of the team, community and in some cases country. They are part of a whole. Their desire and choice in the football game is constrained by their commitment to a consensual agreement pre-determined about how the match should be played to realise a particular goal. Each player is interdependent and has to perform well so that the entire whole can receive maximum satisfaction from the collective goals or results being pursued.

General Systems Theory, which originated from the works of Ludwig von Bertalannfy, is philosophically principled on the aforementioned type of conformity outlined in the previous paragraph. Spruill, Kenney and Kaplan (2001) say that the idea of the whole being more than the sum of its parts dates as far back as Aristotle. General Systems Theory is one of the theories that will be utilised in informing the analysis and conclusions to be discussed later on in this chapter. This theory is broadly applied to various disciplines and is useful because it recognises an intersection among all things as living, interacting with matters of different make-up and the need to pool from various disciplines to make a system work. This intersection is similar to the policy and advocacy convergence being sought with culture, playing football and community development in GAT. This intersection is a point for unification that can be proposed for achieving community development. This looks promising but may be challenging to achieve if the right principles to outline frameworks to be used cannot be identified. General Systems Theory is a shift from the mechanistic, atomic way of studying just individual parts that make up a system. The theoretical assumption is that parts of a system lose their fundamental properties characteristic of the system, when they are taken apart. A system cannot be understood through mechanistic analysis. The goal of using systems thinking in a community setting is to have "community participants shift from being reactors, to viewing themselves as shaping their reality and the future" (Spruill, Kenney & Kaplan, 2001, 108).

Social learning is another theoretical lens being used to understand the issues concerning the intersecting relationship between culture, the playing of football and community development. As earlier described, culture is multifaceted. It can be transmitted through systems such as households, families, community and the society in primary and secondary socialisation processes. Through interaction and learning in these spheres, people see themselves through the eyes of others, become inducted and conscious of roles and how they should function with other members within their systems. There is meaning attached to how people view themselves and the symbols others assign to them. All of this is to a large extent the underlying drivers for the self and collective efficacy they exercise. Self-efficacy is concerned with the level of confidence that persons believe they have in their ability to execute a course of action or attain specific performance outcomes (Roos, Potgieter & Temane, 2013). This assertion of confidence impacts their human functioning in a number of ways. High self-efficacy corresponds positively with high self-esteem, better physical conditions and greater well-being. Collective efficacy is utilised to determine motivational beliefs in groups rather than in individuals. Bandura (1997) suggests that collective efficacy is concerned with shared beliefs in the conjoint strengths that individuals possess to execute courses of action required to achieve designated goals.

Methods
Data Collection
The research conducted was phenomenological and focused on understanding the shared experiences of playing football in GAT. Eight in-depth interviews, focus group and community-wide data mapping and participant observations were conducted. Secondary data were collected about the community and the people.

The main research questions to be answered were:
(1) What has been the experience of playing football in GAT?
(2) How has the experience of playing football in GAT changed?
(3) How has the playing of football brought about community
    development?
Interviewees viewed the question schedule prior to the interview to encourage comfort with answering the questions and opportunity to

provide accurate information and thick, rich descriptions or multiple responses (Dilley, 2000). Interviewees were given a letter of invitation and consent form prior to the interview which outlined the purpose of the study, its owners and the use of the findings. Member checking was done at the end of every interview.

Two focus groups, facilitated by an expert in qualitative research, were done with young males who play for the GAT Under-17 football team. The focus groups assisted with the further validation of information (Creswell & Miller, 2000).

The community-wide data collection process involved visiting five districts known for playing football. Community liaisons assisted in the data collection over six evenings. Residents were more willing to entertain questions because they knew the community liaisons and saw them as one of their own. Liaisons also assisted with communication barriers (e.g. illiteracy) by speaking to the residents in a language they knew and understood.

Residents were interviewed in their setting – in a yard, near a bar, playing dominoes, or sitting on the corner, on their way from work – which gave the researchers an understanding of the social and cultural contexts of the residents. Table 1 captures some observations of various districts. Participatory Learning and Action (PLA) techniques were integrated in the semi-structured interviews that were conducted with approximately 30 individuals. Timelines to capture change in the community, listing with ranking to identify problems and problem and solutions trees were utilised to gather information.

Data Analysis

Following the transcription of data from the eight tape-recorded interviews, transcripts were uploaded to Atlas-ti research software for a first round of open coding. Saldana (2008, 3) explains that:

> A code in qualitative inquiry is most often a word or short phrase that symbolically assigns a summative, salient, essence capturing and/or evocative attribute for a portion of language based or visual data.

Group A-2 Community Districts	Group B-3 Community Districts	Group C-1 Community Districts
Unemployment	Unemployment	Unemployment
Reported violence	Reported violence	No incidence of collective violence relative to A & B
Gang activities	Medium levels of education	Tertiary education
Low levels of education	Gang activities	Unknown gang activities
Poor housing stock	Good housing stock	Recreational facilities/areas
One recreation area	One recreational facility/area	A community meeting place
Small shops	Community meeting place	Community groups
Minimal lighting	One community group	Minimal lighting
More dirt tracks than primary roads	A number of churches	Dusty, narrow roads
	Minimal lighting	

Table 1. Key Community Features Observed in Community-Wide Data Collection

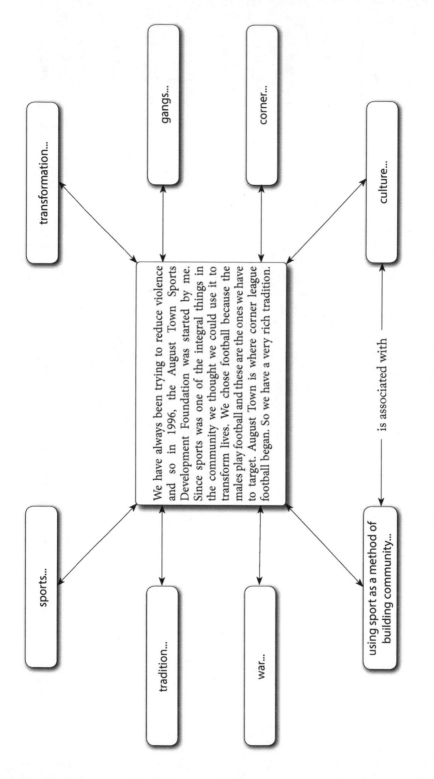

Fig.1 : The Co-occurrences of Different Themed Information

transformation...

gangs...

corner...

culture...

sports...

tradition...

war...

using sport as a method of building community...

is associated with

We have always been trying to reduce violence and so in 1996, the August Town Sports Development Foundation was started by me. Since sports was one of the integral things in the community we thought we could use it to transform lives. We chose football because the males play football and these are the ones we have to target. August Town is where corner league football began. So we have a very rich tradition.

The open round of coding resulted in the generation of several codes and was followed by a selective coding process. Codes with lower frequency of textural descriptions were examined for co-occurrences with other pieces of information and, where suitable, subsumed under that code. Fig.1 shows an example of where a piece of themed information was associated with other themes of information. Where this was not possible, these codes were treated as minor themes of information. The major codes formed the themed information for the write up.

Findings and Discussion

The purpose of this chapter is to explore the relationship between culture, playing football and community development in GAT to determine how the playing of football was part of the normative behaviour and practices of people in the community. Also, how this capital that they possess could be translated into social and economic returns, which could develop the community. The themes of information captured in the interviews revealed several considerations.

People will support their own

The playing of football in GAT was started by one man in the 1970s who thought it was necessary to give the young persons in the community something to do. He wanted to create something that would bring the people closer. After witnessing and experiencing the playing of tennis and football at the nearby UWI, he became interested in introducing football to the community. With one ball, which served the entire community, he began what still prevails today, corner league football. The matches were held among the corners in the community and brought residents together to watch the matches and cheer for their respective teams. The violence was not as pronounced then as it would later become in the 1980s when the founder of corner league football in the community was no longer leading the sport. By that time it was receiving the attention of outside clubs and individuals interested in participating or playing with the teams.

Corner league football was the platform for recruiting persons into playing football for the community. It provided mobility that was characterised by players feeling proud to represent their community and gaining some economic return. By the 1990s, large-scale community violence associated with representational politics dented recruitment in the playing of football for the community beyond the corner league level and this was partly because of young males falling victim to the violence.

Residents interviewed in the community-wide data collection, recalled the period when the "violence had even become part of the playing of football. Some players used the playing of football as the opportunity to settle grudges with other players belonging to different corners." This finding is corroborated by Charles (2004) who found that disagreements over a woman could lead to a confrontation on the football field which escalated into inter-gang violence. Still, being a footballer in the community, especially one playing for the community team carries with it a particular stature and one interviewee recalled that "footballers can travel anywhere in the community, and are not restricted by the rules on crossing boundaries."

The concept of people supporting their own was an interesting element of the analysis for some specific reasons. In the focus groups with the males comprising the Under-17 team, it was revealed that there was not much of the fanfare associated with playing for the senior team of the community. There is not as much recognition by the community, one player noted, of players on the team. In a visit to one of the Under-17 matches, there were very few supporters as compared to the supporter base for the senior team on any given day of their matches. In 2006, the senior team made it to the Premier League games, one of the highest levels of national football championships. This achievement brought a lot pride for the community and esteem to residents and some residents travelled with the team wherever they went to play local matches. It is interesting to note that only two players on the senior team come from the community. During the community-wide data collection, a few residents voiced their dissatisfaction with the membership of the team, indicating that this was one of the reasons they did not go to matches.

The sense of pride, esteem and loyalty of being associated with the football team is not an uncommon experience in other parts of the world. Bob, Swart and Knott (2011) highlight several benefits that communities receive from their participation in sport. These are enhanced employability and community capacity, improvements in health, increased self-esteem and confidence because residents feel empowered. In addition, confidence and self-esteem can be regarded as individual benefits but can be extended to the community in several ways. The reduction in crime in GAT could be seen as consequential of strong sporting activity. This notion is congruent with other expression from interviewees about how the playing of football facilitates a rapport between the police and the at-risk young males in the community. One interviewee described the experience as one where the males enjoyed winning and "beating up the police." The playing of football allows the males to vent and de-stress, one interviewee who is part of the effort to engage young at-risk males in the community said. The playing of football between the police and the at-risk males provided a platform for communication and an avenue for the males to learn more about the police and vice-versa. In one district, residents interviewed said that when corner league football matches were in progress there was no violence in the community.

Transference

As Fig.1 illustrates, there are several themes of information that emerge when one begins to talk about the playing of football in GAT. For instance it is accepted that when you talk about reducing violence in the community sports is included in the conversation. As aforementioned, sports has a historical significance for the community and this was more apparent in the two focus group discussions when the young males were asked how they got into playing football. Their responses included, "introduced to it by my mother," "my father was a footballer," "my grandfather was a footballer," "exposed to the game by older siblings" and "seeing it on television at home."

While we were not able to quantify the psycho-social personal development outcomes emanating from the playing of football by the youth, it was derived that the playing of football has fostered unity even off the field among some of the males. When probed about changes in their behaviour that they had noticed since joining the football team, the males acknowledged that they had an appreciation for discipline and teamwork as these were valuable attributes corresponding with what was needed in the workplace. One youth saw it as fostering qualities that would be needed for achieving an educational scholarship. The youth also saw the playing of football as a chance for achieving social mobility by earning an income from it so that he could open a business to help his mother, father or siblings. We were unable to identify if these life skills were experienced by males playing football in a less structured, competitive manner but we noticed that during the community-wide data collection, there were groups of males who came together on afternoons to play the sport, suggestive of some degree of connectedness and camaraderie.

There is a fair amount of literature and practice supporting the teaching of life-skills to youth through sport or specifically the playing of football. Citing a study done in Tanzania that involved a control and comparative group, Moore (2012) contends that sports can be used to deliver valuable lessons to children on topics such as HIV/AIDS. One of the findings of the Tanzania study showed that children learnt better in a sport setting than in a normal setting, reinforcing the notion that utilising sports can enhance achievements towards community development. Citing another study done in Northern Cambodia, Moore (2012) notes that the researchers agree on the impact sport can have on social cohesion within a community, but sport alone will not solve the challenges faced by a community.

The theme of transference is a very problematic one in the examination of playing football, culture and community development in GAT. It is a problematic concept because there is only a small spill-over of the values associated with football that can also drive community development in the actions and organisation of certain practices in the community. Having established that playing football in the community is a shared experience of many, resources and the management of its playing are lingering challenges. Listed below are a few of the complexities which we have encountered in probing the theme of transference.

(1) The structure of playing football empowers players and those closely related to it to act. But, more than 80 percent of the players are not from the community, so the skills, knowledge and

money that could contribute to the community goes elsewhere. Not to mention the efficacy that can be transferred to others, inspiring them to believe that they, too, can make a contribution to the development of the community.

(2) People come out in droves to watch corner league matches and use these periods as moments to reconcile and share with other members of the community. Yet, these corners have a history of fighting with one another. This reinforces the experience of people who remain connected through particular institutions in society but do not necessarily do so across other structures of their way of life. Residents still locate themselves within a particular district and not with the whole community.

(3) No district has a proper playing field capable of becoming economic capital for the community. There is also an absence of centralisation in leadership among the various organisers of the corner league matches to facilitate the upgrade of a standard facility which could benefit the community team and corner league football playing. The community team utilises a field and other facilities for training located at the UWI. The playing of football in the community has realms, but there is fragmentation with the approaches to playing it and this impedes the capitalisation of the various modes and means of localising production of the football experience in GAT. The successful localisation could bring economic, social and infrastructural development in the community. Bob, Swart and Knott (2011) have said that policy makers do recognise sports for development as a tool that can contribute to countries attainment of the Millennium Development Goals of eradicating poverty, hunger and the promotion of environmental sustainability.

Conclusion

The point at which the playing of football and the community working as a single unit intersects can be a catalyst for people helping to improve the lives of people. The community has a positive history where the playing of football is concerned and it is part of its way of life. However, there are some readiness issues which can only be solved by the community members. For instance, each district operating in isolation of each other creates a barrier to progress in adding value to their sporting and economic capital. As long as we are talking about people improving the lives of each other, change processes, and interdisciplinary approaches, a shift must also take place in the participation of both men and women in the playing of football. The playing of football was an activity for the men, while the females participated in sports such as netball or stayed on the periphery of the game as spectators or vendors during matches. One female, however, was part of the management team of one of the community's football clubs. While it was noted by a few of the young males the significance of their mothers introducing them to the sport, it is also equally important that in one district the women referred to the playing field as belonging to the males. The study did not probe the role allocation of gender in the playing of football in the community and so it is difficult to determine correspondence with societal values. But the absence of overt, active involvement by women in the playing of football may suggest a domesticated type of involvement. That is an important contribution but there may also be more gains from them being at the forefront in the playing of football. The experience of playing football in the community and the role of women is not comparative with the experience of Jamaica and women playing football. As was discussed in chapter 2, the country has a female football team, a female football league and there are also female football teams at the various schools and universities in the country.

The intersection between playing football, community development and culture can only be realised if certain socio-cultural barriers are removed. Violence in the community has torn persons apart and cemented feelings of mistrust and there is not much evidence of restorative points reflective of reconciliation that can allow a new platform to be built for relationships and further networking. This violence and mistrust was also seen in the run up to the 2014 World Cup in Brazil. The socio-economic barriers that excluded millions in Brazil were reinforced even as the country was achieving economic development. There were violent demonstrations about the cost of the World Cup and cost overruns at a time when there were huge inequalities in the society. These issues are explored in the next chapter in terms of what the Caribbean can learn from the experience of Brazil.

Chapter 4

Social Unrests and the 2014 World Cup in Brazil
Lessons for the Caribbean

Basil Wilson

Introduction

It is certainly not happenstance that four countries China, South Africa, Russia and Brazil have recently staged world athletic events. China was the host of the Olympic Games in 2008. South Africa held the World Cup in 2010. Russia was the host of the Winter Olympics in 2014 and Brazil was the host for the World Cup in 2014 and will stage the Olympics in 2016.

Brazil, Russia, India, China and South Africa (BRICS) are countries recognised as rising political and economic powers (Nye, 2011). Staging a world athletic event is an acknowledgement on the part of the host country that the necessary developmental stage has been achieved and the financial resources and organisational skills exist to successfully manage a complex and intricate world event.

These global sporting events are very costly. The 2014 Winter Games in Sochi, Russia, was estimated to cost over $51 billion dollars and Vladimir Putin, president of Russia, saw the staging of the event as a demonstration to the world that Russia is still a great power. There was a rush to get the infrastructure in place on time. There was the fear of terrorism but in the end the games were a success. Putin's successful staging of the Winter Olympics has been over-shadowed by the crisis in the Ukraine and Russia's annexation of Crimea.

The Chinese staging of the summer Olympics in 2008 did not appear to have an adverse effect on domestic fissures in China but it brought international prestige to the Chinese government. Nonetheless, the smog and environmental abuses also revealed that China is facing serious challenges in the decades ahead.

Brazil has been for decades the dominant power in South America and with fairly remarkable economic growth in the latter part of the twentieth century. At the beginning of the twenty-first century, Brazil now seeks recognition as a world power. Brazil has long since been recognised as a power in the world of football. They have won the World Cup five times and playing at home in 2014, the expectation in Brazil was that they would have won their sixth World Cup. Not only did they lose but the 7-1 trouncing by Germany in the semi-final revealed that Brazil has fallen behind in the world of football. This chapter looks at the social protests against the World Cup in Brazil and what Caribbean countries can learn from the events in Brazil in 2014 in terms of how to manage development and change.

The Globalisation of Football

In the world of football, Brazil has become one of the leading exporters of footballing talent. In the era of Edson Arantes do Nascimento (Pelé), most top Brazilian footballers played at home and the national team was selected from home-based players. That is no longer the case in the world of football. The game of football has become a globalised sport and the outstanding talent from all over the world are scouted and selected to play in the highly competitive leagues such as the Barclay's Premier League in England, La Liga in Spain, Serie A in Italy, and the Bundesliga in Germany.

With the globalisation of football, income inequality among clubs has divided leagues into the haves and the have-nots. In Spain, the money clubs are Barcelona and Real Madrid although in the season 2013-2014, Atletico Madrid has emerged as competitor to Barcelona and Real Madrid but they lack the financial depth of a super club. This is illustrated by the fact that at the end of the season the key players that led them to win La Liga were sold to the super clubs.

Bayern-Munich of Germany is one of the richest clubs in the world. American businessmen, for the first time, purchased Roma in Italy. The economy of Italy has fallen on hard times, thus powerful clubs like A.C. Milan and Inter-Milan have had to cut back on the acquisition of expensive players. The acquisition of big name players is where the chasm between the haves and the have-nots is most salient.

Six of the 20 English Premier League teams have been acquired by American millionaire investors. Manchester United, Arsenal,

Sunderland, Aston Villa, Fulham and Liverpool are controlled by American multi-millionaires yet not all of those clubs have been successful in putting together competitive teams. Fulham was demoted to a lower division at the end of the 2013-2014 season. Aston Villa has been on a rebuilding mode and has not spent lavishly. Manchester United and Liverpool have been successful. Liverpool was in contention to win the English Premier League in 2013-2014. Both Liverpool and Manchester United spent lavishly in the summer of 2014 to enhance their chances for the 2014-2015 football season.

In the world of European football, the national leagues have remained significant but the prestige and money are in the Union of European Football Associations (UEFA) Champion's League which encompasses the top European Clubs. That is where the power of money becomes apparent. The clubs competing in the UEFA Champions League are generously endowed such as Chelsea which is owned by the Russian billionaire, Roman Abramovich. Manchester United is owned by the late American billionaire Malcolm Glazer. Manchester City is owned by billionaires from Abu Dhabi. Arsenal, owned by American multi-millionaires, rounds out the top tier group that qualified to play in the Champion's League for last season.

Poor clubs like West Bromwich Albion, Sunderland, Fulham, Norwich and Crystal Palace are like yo-yos. One year they are promoted to the Barclay's Premier League and the next year they are relegated to the lower league where television royalties are not as lucrative. The better players leave to seek their fortunes in the Premier League. Football is no longer the sport of paupers but a highly globalised sport drawing on talent globally and the principal clubs are run by billionaires from all over the world (Gerronel, 2013).

Brazil and the World Cup of 2014

Brazil, as previously mentioned, has become an exporter of football talent to the rich European leagues where salaries are much more lucrative than are paid to players in the Brazilian professional league. The return of Ronaldinho to Brazil and Alexandre Pato of A.C. Milan to Corinthians reflect the desire of Brazilian clubs to recruit talent abroad and keep talent at home. Although Brazilian clubs have increased their revenue with new television contracts, many of the clubs have had trouble keeping up with payments to their professionals.

Ronaldinho has been involved in negotiating back payment for teammates at Atletico Mineiro. Corinthians fell behind in their payment to Alexandre Pato. The globalisation of football has made it difficult for the Brazilian professional league to retain top players like Neymar who migrated to Barcelona for huge transfer fees paid to Santos. In yesteryear, Brazil was able to keep Pelé at home but the departure of Neymar is a manifestation of the power of money in the world of football. Moneywise, the Brazilian league cannot compete with the rich European leagues. There is that stark inequality. Nonetheless, the staging of the World Cup triggered unrest in Brazilian society despite the Brazilian government's progress in reducing the income inequality gap.

Brazil and Income Inequality
Central American and South American economies have been plagued with the concentration of wealth at the top. Income inequality which is measured by the Gini Index is also a serious problem in certain parts of Africa. Based on the calculations of the *CIA World Factbook* the six most egregious countries vis-à-vis income inequality are in Africa. Next in line are the countries in Central and South America. Brazil in 2012 had a Gini Index of 51.9 and was ranked 17th in the world. Honduras was 55.9, Colombia 55.9, Guatemala 55.1, Paraguay 53.2, Bolivia 53.00, Chile 52.1 and Panama 51.9 (CIA, 2013; Ferrara, 2010).

Latin America, in recent decades, has moved away from military dictatorship to a democratic mode of government but the new social democratic order has a long way to go before wealth distribution looks similar to what is extant in the Scandinavian countries. Brazilian democracy is now firmly intact but much of the atavisms of the past persist and glaring poverty is still highly visible in the favelas of cities like Rio de Janeiro and Sao Paulo.

A Synopsis of Brazil's Political History
Brazil's early political history has been tempestuous. Over the decades, there have been vacillations concerning whether the political system

should be centralised or decentralised. Should the states control the federal government or should the federal government be in a position to exercise hegemony. The vacillation in the political system invariably led to much confusion as to whether Brazil was to pursue a state-centric economic development strategy or a laissez-faire form of economic development (Ito, 1999).

In the early decades of the twentieth century, the land-owning class was able to exercise political dominance but as Brazil urbanised, the trade unions were able to flex some level of class interest. In the 1930s, Integralism emerged as a significant political force and was spearheaded by Salgado and Barroso. The Integralist Movement had a fascist orientation. In the 1930s, GetulioVargas with support from the Integralists, emerged as the dominant political figure in Brazil. But, by 1937, he suppressed them and began consolidating power for himself. Vargas defined himself as a corporatist and favoured strong centralised planning of the economy (Ito, 1999).

In much of the twentieth century, the Brazilian military was not reluctant to enter the political arena. The military was uneasy with Vargas' cosy relationship with the Soviet Union and in 1946 thwarted Vargas from putting up himself for re-election. Eurico Dutra who had the support of Vargas ran and won. Nonetheless, Vargas remained a popular political figure and was elected to the presidency in 1951 under free elections. He escaped an assassination attempt engineered by his own inner circle of bodyguards. When evidence surfaced of widespread corruption, he resigned and facing corruption charges he committed suicide (Antunes, 2013; Ito, 1999).

The instability of Brazilian politics was self-evident when Juscelino Kubitschek was elected to the presidential office in 1956 and the construction of the new capital, Brasilia, was embroiled in corruption. Janio Quadros was elected to the presidency in 1961 and after his failure to obtain additional powers from the federal legislature, he opted to resign. The vice-president, Juan Goulart, with greater political appeal, assumed the presidency. Goulart had populist predispositions and in 1964 chose to arm the trade unionists. The Brazilian military left the barracks, took control of the government and remained in power for 20 years (Ito, 1999).

The military was instrumental in opening the economy. Foreign and domestic investments bolstered the economy and this 20-year period is often characterised as the "miracle age" as the economy grew at an accelerated pace. The military returned to their barracks in 1984 and a new federal constitution was ratified in 1988. During the 1990s, Fernando Collor was the political figure at the helm. The economy was plagued with run-away inflation and his minister of finance, Fernando Cardoso, initiated the plano real, a new currency buttressed by tight monetary policy which was instrumental in rolling back hyper-inflation. That initiative enabled Cardoso to defeat Luis Inacio Lula da Silva in the election of 1998. Lula was a perennial candidate in the 1990s and ultimately triumphed at the polls in 2002 and continued the development of the Brazilian economy (Condato, 2006).

The Brazilian Economy
As stated previously, during the military dictatorship from 1964 to 1984, the Brazilian economy grew rapidly. An industrial base was firmly established. During the twenty-first century, the Brazilian economy grew at an average GDP rate of 7.5 percent until 2008 when the collapse of the financial sector in the United States dragged the world economy into The Great Recession and growth was decelerated. Nonetheless, the middle class in Brazil has grown and the appetite for consumption has exploded. Extreme poverty declined from 21 percent in 2003 to 11 percent in 2009 (Ferrara de Souza, 2010; Ferreira, Velez & de Barros; 2004).

Some progress has been made in reducing income inequality. In 2001 to 2009 income growth of the lowest 10 percent grew at 7 percent per annum and the richest 10 percent only increased by 1.7 percent (World Bank, 2013). The Gini Index is at a 50 year low. Brazil's Gini Index was as high as .64 in the 1980s and has come down to .519, some improvement but still high for a middle-income country in which social democrats exercise political hegemony (Ferrara, 2010; World Bank, 2013). The macro-economic indicators remain strong. Brazil's debt to GDP ratio is 58 percent. Unemployment is at 5.2 percent and inflation is at 5.4 percent (World Bank, 2013).

Lula and the Brazilian Safety-Net

"Lula" Ignacio da Silva served two terms as president from 2001 to 2010. Lula has remained a popular political figure and it was his stature that was instrumental in Dilma Rousseff winning the election in 2011. Dilma Rousseff ran for re-election against Maria Silva, Aécio da Cunha and eight other presidential candidates on October 5, 2014. Rousseff came in first and Cunha second. There was a runoff on October 26, 2014, since neither the first nor second place candidate had got more than 51 percent of the votes. Rousseff won.

Under "Lula", Bolsa Familia, a cash programme for mothers to keep their children in school, was designed to break the cycle of poverty. Bolsa Familia reached over 12 million homes and is credited with reducing extreme poverty (Luna, 2010). During Lula's presidency, 30 million people entered the ranks of the middle class and 19 million were lifted from extreme poverty, but many still remained in poverty while a lot of money was spent on the World Cup (Perro, 2004).

Expenditures for the World Cup 2014

Despite all these changes, there remains an underlying discontent that has received new impetus since the preparation began around the World Cup of 2014. New stadia had to be constructed and old stadia had to be refurbished. Many of the stadia ran over budget. The increase in bus fares served as a catalyst for a protest movement coinciding with the holding of the Confederation Cup in the summer of 2013. Working class Brazilians vehemently objected to the $12 billion spent on the World Cup, while the need to build affordable housing and affordable public transportation were being neglected.

Protests took place in Sao Paulo and Rio de Janeiro and also in smaller cities like Porto Alegre in the southern part of Brazil and in Guiania in the central region and in Nata in the northeast of Brazil. In both Sao Paulo and Rio de Janeiro, protesters clashed with the police who used tear gas and rubber bullets to break up the demonstrations. The Rousseff Administration astutely rolled back the fare increases in public transportation and promised improved services from the government vis-à-vis education and housing (Bonater, 2013).

The Police and the Favelas

The favelas are the outgrowth of the massive influx of people from the rural areas into the cities. With the dearth of affordable housing, favelas sprung up all over Sao Paulo and Rio de Janeiro. In Rio de Janeiro there are approximately 763 favelas (Bonater, 2013). Relationships between the communities in the favelas and the police have always been frayed. In conjunction with the World Cup of 2014 and the Olympics of 2016, the Brazilian government has embarked on a policy to integrate the favelas into the larger society. The Rousseff Administration's strategy for the favelas is called the Urban Pacification Programme which entails the police taking control of favelas and driving out drug traffickers whose influence on these communities (Bonater, 2013) is similar to the power wielded by the drug cartels in parts of Mexico and the dons in the garrison communities of Jamaica (Charles, 2002, 2004; Charles & Beckford, 2012). The Pacifying Police Unit (UPP) has worked well in some favelas like Santa Marta, but in a huge favela like Rocinha with over 100,000 squatters, the police have met with stiff resistance (Bonater, 2013; Romero, 2014b).

Brazil's police pre-date the advent of democracy. The police training and organisational structure is more congruent with a military rather than a civilian police force. They function under military rules and military discipline but they are not part of the Brazilian military. The Brazilian police have a reputation for ruthlessness. On an average, the police kill five persons per day. In 2013, 1,890 civilians were killed by the police, 351 of those deaths occurred in Sao Paulo (Barbara, 2014). There is an undeclared war between the police and organised crime groups in the favelas and there have been persistent allegations that the police possess an underground death squad (Barbara, 2014). An average of 100 police officers are killed while on duty every year.

One sees the reliance on extra-judicial killings rather than the processing of suspects through the established criminal justice system. In the early part of 2014, in the city of Campinas, a police officer was shot and killed in a robbery in the presence of his wife. Within hours, 12 people were rounded up and executed gangland style. The extra-judicial killings have worked at cross purposes with the government's objective to integrate the favelas into the larger society. The pacification programme has met resistance from organised crime groups and police-community relations have been exacerbated by the extra-judicial killings and the rampant abuse of power (Barbara, 2014).

In Rocinha, the police killing of a construction worker precipitated large-scale protest. The resident, De Souza, was arrested, tortured and died in police custody. After a thorough investigation, the police officer in charge of the pacification programme for Rocinha was arrested along with other police officers (Romero & Barnes, 2014).

In Rio de Janeiro, in the north, at the Manguindo complex of favelas, drug traffickers have been having shoot-outs with the police. The situation has become so precarious that the governor of Rio de Janeiro, Sergio Cabral, requested that President Rousseff send in the army because the police were being overwhelmed. The President obliged but that act of desperation and the shakiness of the social order in the favelas meant that the World Cup 2014 was held in circumstances not far from a state of emergency (Reuters, 2014).

The Brazilian coercive apparatus in the midst of World Cup 2014 preparations had to deal with mass demonstrations against corruption and other social and political grievances and concomitantly try to simmer the smouldering situation in the favelas. To further complicate the social unrest, a non-political non-insurgency movement known as the Rolezinhos has emerged. Young people, mostly Black, come together through social media and thousands gather and rampage through upscale shopping malls. Apparently, the teenagers see the invasion of elite shopping malls as a form of protest against the race and class prejudice still rampant in Brazilian society. In response, the shopping mall owners and store owners out of fear shut down malls when the protesters gather and are out to invade (Romero, 2014a).

The Rolezinhos are not explicitly political. But, it is a manifestation of the still rigid class barriers that have always been an integral part of Brazilian society. As the middle class has expanded and extreme poverty has diminished, the Rolezinho represents a social movement aimed at breaking down race and class barriers in Brazil's tempestuous urban society. Rolezinhos, a new social phenomenon, is a response by thousands of socially excluded Black teenagers anxious to showcase name brand clothing. They could be politicised if they become subject to police brutality and are insulted by segregated malls that have become the preserve of the rich and the upper middle class (Romero, 2014a).

Conclusion – the World Cup in Perspective with Caribbean Lessons

The World Cup 2014 was in many respects Brazil's coming of age party as a world power. However, the hosting of the competition triggered unintended socio-economic and political consequences. The construction of stadia and infra-structural development stimulated economic activities. But the World Cup spectacle has also meant the coming out party for voices that have been traditionally silent such as the voices from the favelas, the Rolezinhos, and other Black urban youths.

The Caribbean which is in love with the Brazilian style of football is struggling economically and should learn from the events in Brazil. Economic development in the Caribbean should be inclusive especially for groups that have been historically marginalised. Moreover, these and other groups are not going to tolerate massive government funding for football or other sports when there are several competing societal issues for the funds.

The last three presidential elections have been won by the Workers Party of Brazil. That party is symbolised by Lula da Silva who is the most popular politician in Brazil. The Workers Party is committed to economic change and closing the gap of income inequality in Brazil. The expansion of the middle class and the reduction of extreme poverty have not brought stability to Brazilian society. Much progress has been made but there are still large numbers of citizens that are socially excluded.

The foregoing facts in Brazil suggest that the governments of Caribbean states, when they experience accelerated growth and development must dismantle the barriers to social exclusion. Also, the survival of Caribbean governments not only requires political leaders who connect with the people and are popular but also leaders that are committed to the economic changes that development requires. The building of social capital and effective communication with the people are required to win their support for change and the initial instability that comes with economic changes.

The dialectic between the police and the favelas constitutes a serious challenge to social order in Brazil. Favelas did not emerge overnight and for decades they were neglected and left to fester like a sore. Langston Hughes' poem *Harlem* in which the opening line asks what happens to a dream that is deferred (Hughes, 1990) reflects what has happened in Brazil.

> *What happens to a dream deferred?*
> *Does it dry up*
> *like a raisin in the sun?*
> *Or fester like a sore—*
> *And then run?*
> *Does it stink like rotten meat?*
> *Or crust and sugar over—*
> *like a syrupy sweet?*

Drug trafficking and a sub-culture of violence is deeply rooted in the larger favelas. Even though the UPP is a gallant effort, preliminary attempts to provide the favelas with a police presence and greater amenities have been varied. The militarisation of the Brazilian police has alienated the community in the larger favelas like Rocinha.

It is important that Caribbean states note that it is unwise to deploy law enforcement and develop infrastructure in deprived urban communities controlled by drug gangs solely because a world event of significance is being hosted in the country. The people in these materially deprived communities are going to resist the government which they believe is more interested in protecting the image of the country rather than improving their socio-economic well-being. In addition, effective policing of the poor requires long-standing social capital between the poor and the police. A lack of social capital means that the poor and the police are always going to be in conflict. This trust must be built and the rights of the people respected by the government and the police so that the people are co-opted in support of progress.

The mass demonstrations did not prevent the Confederation Cup or the World Cup from taking place. The great Brazilian footballer

Pelé refers to football as the beautiful game. The beautiful game was initially perfected in Brazil but that style is now played all over the world. Brazil's staging of the World Cup 2014 revealed that the samba nation still has a long way to trod to make the claim that Brazil is a beautiful developed society. What is paradoxical is that Brazil has been dislodged from the pinnacle of world football. The Brazilian national team, the Selectao, was embarrassingly routed by the Germans 7-1 in the World Cup semi-final and lost to the Netherlands 3-0 in the third place play off.

The Brazil experience suggests that Caribbean governments, like their Brazilian counterpart, cannot control and influence how their countries' football teams play in any particular game but they can influence what happens in the economy. The people of a nation that are passionate about football will feel dejected and humiliated when the national football team is trounced at home by an opponent. However, these same people will feel and protest worse when the economy is bad, they believe their government is not making the right economic decisions, or they are at the bottom of the government's priority list.

There has to be changes in Brazilian football if Brazil is to return as a world champion in 2018. In the same vein, Brazil has got to expand affordable housing, improve conditions in the favelas and create a police department worthy of a democratic society. Brazil has emerged as a world power but its internal race and class dynamics cry out for further transformation. Brazil is no longer in the vanguard of world football as the globalisation of the game has left the professional league in Brazil trailing the rich super clubs in Europe, in the same way that globalisation has created inequality in the world community.

Caribbean governments have to be mindful about how globalisation impacts the development of their economies and football among other sports. The football clubs in the Caribbean when they are professionalised will be at a huge disadvantage economically compared to the European clubs. The priority of club owners will be to engage globalisation in ways that develop the clubs and maximise profits. The development of football in the region requires that commensurate development occurs in communities, especially those that are experiencing poverty. This balance is of critical importance if the government is to govern change effectively without social disorder. The next chapter deals the phenomenal Caribbean footballer, the biracial Andrew Watson of British Guiana, who was one of the world's greatest players of the modern game. Watson had to balance his love for the game and the racism that he navigated daily in England and Scotland.

Chapter 5

Andrew Watson:
The Caribbean Football Pioneer of the Modern Game

Tony Talburt

Introduction

The Anglophone Caribbean has produced some sporting legends over the years. In the sport of cricket one could mention Sir Garfield Sobers, Clive Lloyd and Brian Lara as examples of superstars. Similarly, the Jamaican athletes Arthur Wint, Herb McKenley and Usain Bolt certainly stand out as extraordinary sportsmen. In terms of international netball, some of the Anglophone Caribbean nations such as Barbados, Trinidad and Tobago, and Jamaica are highly rated. With regard to international football, however, the Caribbean region has not had the same level of success. Apart from Dwight York of Trinidad and Tobago, who played for Manchester United at a period when they were considered one of the very best club teams in the world, and Allan Cole of Jamaica who played for top Brazilian club Nautica among others, the Caribbean region is not noted for its ability to produce many footballers of high international standard. Given this situation, it might at first seem paradoxical that this chapter seeks to examine the achievements of one Caribbean-born footballer (Andrew Watson 1856-1921) whose on and off field ability was not only remarkable, but equally of the highest international standards at the time. Watson not only played football in England and Scotland in the 1870s and 1880s, and was probably the world's first Black footballer, he was the world's first Black national football captain. What is even more astonishing is the fact that Watson played and captained the Scottish national football team in 1881 at a time when they were arguably the very best national team in the world.

The purpose of this chapter, therefore, is to examine the extraordinary achievements of this Caribbean-born football genius who was one of the world's greatest players and who, in part at least, was also one of the early pioneers who contributed to the development of the modern game of football in Britain. Although much could be written about his wider social life and his relatively affluent social status within British society during the late nineteenth and early twentieth centuries, this chapter will concentrate primarily on Watson the footballer. It is important to point out that for Watson to have reached the pinnacle of the sport when he did, he must have been an exceptionally talented player, given the virulent racism of the period against Blacks. The chapter first provides a biographical overview of Watson's life and his most significant achievements. Secondly, it examines the importance of the crucial period of the 1870s-1880s when he played and when many essential features of the modern game were being developed. Lastly, the chapter discusses the significance of each of the three main football teams that Watson played for – Queen's Park, Scotland and Corinthians of London – demonstrating how these were, at their peak, the very best teams in Britain.

The essential rationale for this particular chapter arises from the fact that very little has been written about the life and achievements of Watson, especially within the context of individual footballers or Scottish influences, more generally, which contributed to the development of the modern game of football in Britain. Part of what makes this chapter important is the fact that it suggests that Watson not only played football at the highest level during the 1880s, but was doing so at a time when the very nature of some aspects of the game were being radically transformed, developed and ultimately exported to England and the wider world. Moreover, it was during this period that Scotland (where Watson played most of his football) was able to transfer their particular 'passing' style of football to England. That Andrew Watson, who was very definitely an integral part of this Scottish approach, should be either ignored or forgotten is a travesty and makes it necessary that his story be told so he can be remembered and recognised as one of the pioneers during this phase of the development of the modern game of football in Britain.

While the presence of Black players in post-war Britain is fairly commonplace in the modern game, very little has been written about their involvement prior to this period. The few studies which have concentrated on Black footballers have tended to focus on the names Arthur Wharton born in Ghana in 1865 and Walter Tull who was born in Kent, England in 1888. For example, Vasili's work (1998) makes the point, most powerfully, that Wharton was Britain's first Black footballer. What is very interesting about Vasili's study is the fact that a number of other notable White footballers born outside Britain who played at the national level were also highlighted. For example, James Frederick Mcleod Prinsep, who was born in India, was singled out for special mention. He not only played for Clapham Rovers in the 1870s but also had one national cap for England against Scotland in 1879, and was regarded as the youngest player to play for England at the age of 17 (Vasili, 1998). He also mentions two non-white players who played at the national level. The first was Eddie Parris of Bradford who was selected by Wales in 1931 and was the first Black player for the national team. The first non-white player for England was Hong Y 'Frank' Soo who played in 1941 (Vasili, 1998). Interestingly, however, Watson, who not only played for Scotland in 1881, but captained the team which beat England 6-1 (their heaviest defeat on home soil), was not mentioned.

Hamilton and Hinds (1999) made the similar point that among the names of Black footballers who paved the way for later generations were Arthur Wharton and Walter Tull (Hamilton & Hinds, 1999). They, very importantly, mention the significance of other players such as Albert Johanneson and Steve Mokone as examples of Black footballers who played in England in the late 1950s and 1960s (Hamilton & Hinds, 1999). More generally, where studies have examined the origins or development of football in Britain, the same kind of pattern can be observed. For example, Lowndes (1952) mentioned some of the great players of the English game – Steve Bloomer of Derby, Billy Meredith of Manchester City and Peter Doherty of Blackpool and then Manchester City (Lowndes, 1952). In Golesworthy's *Encyclopaedia of Association Football* (1973), under the heading of 'Coloured Players' he noted that Parris who played for Bradford, Luton Town, Northampton Town, Bournemouth and Boscombe Athletic between 1928-1939 was the only 'coloured' player to appear in an international championship.

Two reasons help to explain why Watson's name seems to have been forgotten. Firstly, Watson played at a time when the game was essentially dominated by amateurs. Professional football was formally established in 1885 in England and 1893 in Scotland. Notwithstanding this, he had a most distinguished amateur career playing for the very best amateur clubs in Britain at that time, namely, Queen's Park of Glasgow and Corinthians based in London. While Arthur Wharton can, therefore, be considered as the first Black professional footballer in Britain, Watson very definitely preceded him by at least 12 years since he played for Parkgrove Football club in 1876 and had, in fact, been playing for Maxwell FC from about 1874. Many of the studies on the history of football have tended to place much of their emphasis on the professional game and seem to ignore the very early period before professionalisation.

In addition, most of Watson's football career took place in Scotland, and as the game developed and changed in terms of style and rules in England after the 1880s, Watson's worth, and those of other players north of the border, have received less attention as the game in England began to take pride of place within the British Isles. It is worth noting, as an example of this, that Lowndes (1952) mentioned a stand-out international match between England and Scotland in 1928 when a very good Scotland team completely outplayed England and beat them 5-1. Yet, Scotland's 6-1 victory over England in 1881 was totally ignored, even though this was probably a more significant achievement, particularly since the game was played in London. This achievement makes it even more remarkable that a Black British Guianese-born player could captain the Scottish national team.

The second reason for the dearth of information on Watson was that many of the books on the history of football in Britain have tended to focus on the nature of the changes within the actual game rather than the stand-out personalities who played. For example, Harvey (2005), Mason (1980) and Walvin, (1994b), are good cases in point that examine the general conditions or factors which influenced the development of football in Britain without going into tremendous detail about individual personalities. Their focus has been on the changing nature of the socio-economic conditions, especially among the working class; the impact of the freeing-up of Saturday afternoons as time off for workers, which corresponded with the growth in popularity of Saturday afternoon football games; or the impact of the football played in elite public schools. Many of the individual footballers were not featured.

For example, Walvin's (1994b) focus was on the development of the game by the end of the nineteenth century among the working classes. One of the many reasons cited for this was the increasing acceptance of the idea of Saturday afternoon holiday for workers especially in industrial cities in Britain after the 1860s (Walvin, 1994b). The most obvious consequence of this gradual introduction of the Saturday holiday for workers was that it allowed the workers of industry to participate in organised recreation on their free afternoons (Walvin, 1994b).

Even the very important work by Robinson (1920) on the history of Queen's Park Football Club, which actually mentions the names of team members, does not provide detailed commentary on any individual. For example, he discusses how and when the team was formed in 1867 as well as their main achievements during the first 50 years of their existence. As the different teams and officials during that 50-year period are mentioned, it becomes clear who played for the team and in what year. Only very brief commentaries or annotations are provided about some of the individual players which help to give some details and it is within this context, too, that Watson's name is mentioned as one of the players in the victorious Queen's Park side which had won the Scottish Cup and the Glasgow Charity Cup in the season 1880-1881. In a couple of places (discussed below), Robinson actually comments on Watson's actual playing ability. In general, however, detailed discussions about footballers, especially those outside of England prior to the 1890s, were few and far between.

A Brief Biography of a Caribbean Football Genius

Because the primary purpose of this chapter is to examine the extraordinary achievements of Andrew Watson, it is necessary to provide a brief overview of his life and main achievements as this sets the context for much of the subsequent analysis. Watson's claim to fame can be based on the number of firsts for which he was responsible. He was Scotland's and also Britain's first Black national football captain. He was the first Black man to play for the Scottish national team. He was also the world's first Black football club administrator when he worked as club secretary for Parkgrove and also Queen's Park football clubs. He was the first Black player to win the Scottish Cup three times and the first Black player to play in an English FA Cup game when he played for the English club Swifts FA in 1882. Watson was, therefore, Britain's first Black celebrity footballer. Despite his rather illustrious career, Watson's story had more humble beginnings thousands of miles away on the South American mainland colony of British Guiana.

Andrew Watson was born in Georgetown, British Guiana (hereafter referred to as Guyana) in 1856 to a Scottish plantation owner named Peter Miller Watson and a local Black woman named Hannah Rose. According to the sports historian Andy Mitchell, after Peter Watson's death in 1869, he 'left his children £35,000' which meant Watson (and his sister) had financial security (Mitchell, 2013). Watson's father had sent him and his sister to England to further their education. Andrew Watson was a pupil at the King's College School in London which had been established in 1829 as a junior department of the then newly established King's College, part of the University of London. This was, and still is, a very prestigious school.

That Watson should have received such privileged treatment was not unusual during this period. Because of the tremendous wealth generated by Caribbean plantation owners from Scotland and England, many of them rose in social standing and were able to send their children (especially the boys) to some of the best schools in England and Scotland. Furthermore, it was also becoming increasingly common for Scottish plantation owners to send their children back to Scotland to receive formal education. Many of these children were fathered by White Scots men who had Black mistresses, thus giving rise to the number of "Mulatto" children who later found themselves in Scotland. John Robertson of Tobago for example, paid for the board and lodgings for Charles and Daniel Robertson, two mulatto boys (Hamilton, 2005).

According to Hamilton, 148 students from the Caribbean were enrolled at Eton College between 1753 and 1776, compared with only 22 from the 13 North American colonies (Hamilton, 2005). In addition, he informs us that between 1731 and 1810, 119 students from the Caribbean matriculated at Glasgow University while at Edinburgh, 114 students from the Caribbean graduated in medicine between 1744 and 1810 (Hamilton, 2005). One such son of the Caribbean who went to study in Scotland was, of course, Andrew Watson. In 1875 he moved from London to study mathematics, natural philosophy, and civil engineering at Glasgow University, but after a year he left there to go and work as an engineering apprentice. He married Jessie Armour in 1877 and they had two children. The 1881 census showed that Andrew Watson and his wife and child lived at Afton Crescent in Govan, Scotland.

That Watson's father should be a Scottish man with Caribbean plantation business was also not abnormal during the eighteenth and nineteenth centuries. By the middle of the eighteenth century Scottish towns like Glasgow had flourishing manufacturing industries which were linked to the Caribbean slave trade. In the Glasgow tobacco trades, Caribbean sugar, and cotton trades, there was a corresponding increase in demand for storage and merchandising facilities. In fact between 1765 and 1795, Hamilton claimed there was a ten-fold increase of Scottish linen exports to Jamaica, arising mainly to meet the demand for coarse osnaburg cloth for slave garments (Hamilton, 2005). Furthermore, it appears that there were a considerable number of Scottish plantation owners or overseers and a Scottish community along the Demerara River in Guyana even before the country was ceded to Britain following the Napoleonic wars in 1815.

For Andrew Watson, and Black people in general, living in towns like Glasgow would not have been a totally unusual occurrence. Black people had been present in Scotland from the beginning of the sixteenth century. Walvin (1994a) informs us that there were a number of Africans at the court of King James IV of Scotland about 1500 A.D. Further evidence of the early Black presence in Scotland has also been provided by Fryer who claimed that one of the Africans at this special event was a drummer and choreographer of whom the

King seemed very fond (Fryer, 1984). The Black eighteenth century anti-slavery campaigner and author, Olaudah Equiano had, among his subscribers for the sixth edition of his book in 1793, 487 subscribers in England, 68 in Ireland and 158 in Scotland (Fryer, 1984). This indicates the extent to which the issue of slavery and the campaign against it exercised the minds of significant numbers in Scotland who were certainly aware of the exploitation of many Black people in their presence most of whom also experienced racism.

Watson's football career in Scotland started when he played for the Scottish senior club called Parkgrove and by 1876 his brilliance became apparent to those involved in the game. He was later invited to join Scotland's most famous amateur club, Queen's Park, where, according to Mitchell, his talent gave him a spot on the national team of Scotland in 1880 (Mitchell, 2013). Watson was officially said to have joined the Queen's Park Football Club on April 6, 1880 from Parkgrove Football Club and eventually left for Liverpool on December 1, 1887 (Robinson, 1920).

His first football medal was the Glasgow Charity Cup Final in 1880. In 1881 Watson was selected to captain Scotland and, on his debut, led them to a 6-1 win over England. In the same year he helped his club Queen's Park to win the Scottish Cup. In 1882 he played two more games for Scotland against England and Wales with both games ending 5-1 in Scotland's favour. In 1882 his club team again won the Scottish Cup final. Precisely because he was an amateur player, it was also at this time that Watson decided to move to England to seek further work as both an engineer and also as a footballer, thus, bringing his Scottish national football career to an abrupt end, as only home-based players for Scottish clubs were selected for the national Scottish team.

As was common among amateur footballers, players were virtually free to play for a number of different clubs in the same season. Therefore, for the next three years Watson played for clubs such as the London side Swifts, Brentwood and Pilgrims. His most notable achievement during this period was when he played for and toured with the exclusive London football club called Corinthians. One of his main highlights during his time with them was being part of the team's 8-1 'crushing of the then F.A. Cup holders Blackburn Rovers in

1884. He returned to Glasgow occasionally to play for Queen's Park and helped them to win the Scottish Cup in 1886. This was Watson's third Scottish cup-winners medal.

Watson left Glasgow and returned to England where he played for a team in Liverpool called Bootle FC which was Everton's main rival. According to Mitchell, this team actually provided salaries and signing bonuses to some of the celebrated players and there was no doubt that Watson was one of their key attractions. According to Mitchell, if this could be proved, this would make Watson the first Black professional footballer and not Arthur Wharton who played in 1889.

Watson's first wife Jessie Armour died in 1882. He married again in February 1887 to Elizabeth Kate Tyler. For the next 20 years Watson worked on ships as an engineer and travelled extensively all over the world including Australia and the Americas. By 1892 he had become a second engineer. He eventually settled in the London suburb of Kew at 88 Forest Road and died on March 8, 1921. His body is buried at the Richmond Cemetery where his second wife and their daughter are also buried.

Scottish Contributions to the Development of Football in Britain in the 1870s-1880s

Any discussion or appreciation of Watson's achievements and contributions to the development of football makes it necessary to focus some attention on the impact of Scotland upon the development of British football during the 1870s-1890s. Scotland's role is important for our purposes because it was here that Watson played most of his football and also because he was part of the general wave of Scottish players who had made a significant impact on the way the game would eventually be played in England. These decades were important because they corresponded with a time in Glasgow's history which was accompanied by spectacular economic growth and development (Moorhouse, 1984), which also facilitated the growth in popularity of football among its working classes.

Giulianotti and Robertson's (2009) study, *The Globalization of Football*, notes that the 1870s-1920s was a critical period in the development and spread of football across Europe and the rest of the world. They contend that the game of football has been a highly important aspect of the globalisation process which took place over five phases stretching from the fifteenth century to the twenty-first. The first phase covered the period from the fifteenth to the nineteenth centuries where various forms of football or a game involving the kicking of a ball between two teams or groups, took place in different parts of the world (Giulianotti & Robertson, 2009). The second phase covered the period of the early nineteenth century to 1870 and was characterised by the development of many aspects of the modern game influenced by the social elite in Britain who established the governing rules (Giulianotti & Robertson, 2009). The third phase covered the period from 1870 to the 1920s, while the fourth phase covered the period from the 1920s to the late 1960s which the writers describe as the 'struggle for hegemony' as different countries competed for global dominance of the game in terms of rules, commercial influence and the power and influence of their national players who were regarded as national heroes (Giulianotti & Robertson, 2009). The fifth period covered the years from the 1960s through to the 2000s.

It is, however, the third period from the 1870s which is significant for this chapter. This was the period when football was becoming embedded within the popular cultures of Europe and South America, and in the 'Europeanised' parts of Africa, the Caribbean, Asia and North America (Giulianotti & Robertson, 2009). It is interesting to note, therefore, that at the very time when the sport was being developed and beginning to emerge on the world scene (1870s and 1880s), Scottish influence on the game was at its peak. It is remarkable, then, that Andrew Watson featured significantly during this phase in the development of British football history as one of Britain's best players.

Even though it is generally argued that the modern version of the game we now commonly call football was largely a creation of the English public schools of the nineteenth century, Harvey suggests that this is not the case. For at least 300 years, games were contested with even numbers on each side and regulated by rules (Harvey, 2005). In fact, he claims that from the period 1600 to 1800 football was played in a number of locations within Britain

(Harvey, 2005). What is clear, however, is the fact that by the last quarter of the nineteenth century, the game had become more popular as well as more tightly regulated by a set of common rules. These developments were not without some degree of opposition. According to Mason (1980), the nature of the football game which was played before the last four decades of the nineteenth century was rough and accompanied by degrees of violence and physical injuries during matches. In addition, more and more football was being played on the streets and local parks which resulted in local and national authorities attempting to ban such events. The Highways Act of 1835 prohibited the playing of football on the highways with fines of up to 40 shillings being levied on those caught (Mason, 1980). As late as the year 1911, of the 605 children brought before the Birmingham Juvenile Court, 132 cases were for those accused of playing football in the streets (Mason, 1980). However, nothing, it seems, could prevent the growth of this popular sport.

The increasing popularity of football was accompanied by significant changes in the way the game was played. It was particularly within this context that the influence of Scottish players would affect the development of the game in England. Until the early 1880s, the focus of the annual cup competitions in England was dominated by the 'amateur gentlemen' primarily from the south of the country (Walvin, 1994b). However, partly as a result of Scottish players moving south of the border to play in England and bringing with them much greater skills and a team-approach to the game, they began to influence the way the game was played. Mason also commented on the fact that the borrowing of players from other clubs for important matches became increasingly popular by the end of the 1870s. Such activities were considered by some to be against the spirit of the game, especially when the 'imported professors' came from north of the border (Mason, 1980). Scotland influenced football in England in two inter-related ways; first through the style of play and secondly, through their importation of Scottish footballers in great numbers into English clubs primarily in the north of the country. For much of the two decades from 1870, football was essentially an amateur game played by gentlemen from very privileged socio-economic backgrounds. By the 1890s in both Scotland and England the game had become professional. One of the features of the style of football played especially by the players from the elite universities and schools in the south of England was their emphasis on individual dribbling skills as opposed to the passing of the ball. As Walvin points out, the whole emphasis of the game, then, was to attack, hence most of the players were forwards and dribbling was the norm (Walvin, 1994b). It was in this particular respect that Scotland changed the way the game was played in England. This, as we will see below, was primarily brought about by Scotland's premiere amateur club, Queen's Park, which had been formed in 1867. Andrew Watson was one of the players who played for this team and subsequently moved south to play for English clubs where he would have contributed to this new approach. Unlike the gentlemen footballers of Eton, Harrow and Rugby, the emphasis and general style of football in Scotland was based on a combination of passing as well as dribbling with a strong desire and ambition to play and win as one team.

The fact was that the typical English-style of play up to the 1890s was based on eight attacking players with one defender and one mid-field player adopting a 1-1-8 formation. Such was the emphasis on forward players dribbling their way through to the goal. Queen's Park and the Scottish national team, however, had a different system based on 2-2-6 formation. This would still be considered very attacking by today's standards. However, Queen's Park's approach, at least, had two definite defenders and sometimes three to check the advance of the opposing attackers. It was only by the end of the 1890s that English clubs, primarily those in the north of the country, began to change their style and formations.

Mason informs us that the Scots, particularly those connected to the Queen's Park Football Club, appeared to have pioneered the passing game in the 1870s. When, for example, Queen's Park visited Aston Villa in 1881 (by which time Watson, a defender, was a player at the club) they played as one team. Mason reports from the *Birmingham Daily Mail*, October 21, 1881 that the approach by Queen's Park was not selfish, they dribbled with the ball close to their feet and their passes were accurate, they played their positions well and the back and half back played exceptionally well (Mason, 1980). By the late 1880s Preston North End was arguably the best team in England, and had been influenced in part by the importation of Scottish players who used this combination football incorporating dribbling and passing. Preston North End's dominance of the English game can be seen with reference to the fact that in March 1887, to commemorate Queen Victoria's 50 years on the throne, they were invited to play the elite amateur team Corinthians of London (another elite amateur club) as part of a Festival of Football at the Kennington Oval in London in which both teams played to a 1-1 draw (Vasili, 1998). Over the next few years, Aston Villa and Sunderland who were both dominant in the 1890s could, according to Mason, similarly attribute much of their success to the importation of Scottish players who were particularly skilled in the passing game (Mason, 1980). In this way, Scottish players were able to join and influence or teach the English how to play the passing game. For this reason, the Scots were referred to as the "professors" and Watson, could also be considered as the "Black Scottish professor from Guyana."

As previously mentioned, English clubs in the north of the country, where the game was more advanced than in the south of England, had been keen to 'import' Scottish players. In 1885, there were 58 Scottish footballers playing for English clubs and 57 of them played for teams in Lancashire 'the hotbed of professional football' at that time (Vasili, 1998). In 1884 and 1885 Queen's Park Football Club had reached the finals of the English FA Cup where they were beaten both times by Preston North End. What is worthy of note is the fact that Preston North End beat them 3-0 with the assistance of six expatriates from Scotland (Vasili, 1998). More importantly, within a few years, a number of other English clubs were playing the passing game which had been introduced to them from Scotland. Preston North End was composed mainly of Scottish players, while the first 11 players to play for Liverpool were all Scots (Murray, 1984). The Everton team which won the league title in 1890-91 had four outstanding Scottish players in the team. For the following two seasons, the league was won by a Sunderland team which consisted of 10 Scottish players and even the one Englishman, Tom Porteous, had apparently joined from a

Scottish club (Golesworthy, 1972). Aston Villa was the other team which dominated the English Football League championship in the 1890s and also had five Scottish players in the first team.

At first, the approach by Scotland to infiltrate the English game with their numerous players and then change the style was not always appreciated. For example, When Scotland beat England in 1884, one English reporter complained about the formation of three defenders that the Scots used which had curbed dribbling and scientific strategies (Mason, 1980). Similarly, the importation of Scotsmen to play in the English clubs created some hostilities and negative comments. Mason informs us that in Lancashire by the 1880s they had a number of imported players, playing for local clubs 'not to mention actual paid men', which the FA tried to ban from cup ties in 1882 but this initiative failed (Mason, 1980).

The influence and dominance of Scotland upon English football cannot be denied. For example, the Scottish national team was so strong during the 1870s and 1880s that of the first 15 games between the national teams of England and Scotland from 1872 to the end of the 1880s, only once did England beat Scotland (Vasili, 1998). The dominance of northern clubs, many of which were made up of Scottish players or adopting the Scottish approach, can also be seen from the fact that between 1883 and 1915 it was primarily clubs from the North and the Midlands of England which dominated the FA Cup competitions, winning it 21 times (Walvin, 1994b). Similarly, when the English Football League was formed in 1888 with 12 founding clubs, all of them were from the North and Midlands of England (Walvin, 1994b). A Scotsman, William McGreggor who was based in Birmingham and a key figure in the development of Aston Villa in 1874, was instrumental in the formation of the English Football League in 1888. In the last quarter of the nineteenth century, Scotland's contribution to the development of football in Britain, and subsequently the world, was immense, when taken into consideration the relatively small size of the country compared to England. They influenced the way the game was played by moving from Scotland to play for English clubs and helped to transform the style of play. Watson was a key member of the successful Queen's Park team and also moved south where, as we saw earlier, he played for a number of different clubs in England. If it is generally accepted that 'Scottish professors' were pioneers in the development of the modern game through helping to influence and transform the nature of the English game in the last quarter of the nineteenth century, then certainly, Andrew Watson, on this basis alone should be considered as one of these pioneers. Further testimony to this fact can also be seen from the quality of the teams he played for. This is the basis of the final section of this chapter.

Watson - A World-class Player

Andrew Watson's football career was remarkable on a number of accounts, but none more so than the fact that he played for the best national team as well as the two best club teams in Britain. Given the fact that there were no other teams playing at such advanced levels at that time, this means Watson was actually playing football for the very best teams in the world. This section looks at the significance of these three teams for which Watson was a key player; the first was Queen's Park, second, Scotland and third Corinthians of London.

One of the salient features of Scottish football since the 1860s, which is in stark contrast to the game in England, has been the extent to which only three teams have dominated their game. The nature and significance of Scottish football in the 1870s and 1880s was dominated by Queen's Park Football Club as it is today dominated by Celtic and Rangers. The domination of these two latter clubs can be demonstrated by the fact that between the years 1891 and 1983, excluding the war years of 1914-1918 and 1940-1947, these two clubs won the Scottish Championship 64 times between them. Furthermore, up to the year 1980, 112 Rangers players were capped for Scotland, compared to 87 Celtic players and 27 from Aberdeen (Moorhouse, 1984). What is particularly significant for this chapter is the fact that when Queen's Park Club was at its zenith in the early to mid-1880s, Andrew Watson was one of their star players.

The significance of Queen's Park Football Club to Scottish and indirectly British football cannot be underestimated. According to Robinson, Queen's Park was responsible for the development of football in Scotland, the Scottish Football Association Code, and ultimately, the very style of play based on the passing-game (Robinson, 1920). The aim or purpose of this amateur club was, from the beginning, for the 'amusement and recreation of its members' (Robinson, 1920, 48). It would remain an amateur club while most of the other clubs around them, which developed later, eventually became professional and thus eventually took centre stage in terms of dominating Scottish football. Although they were an amateur football club, their standard and quality of football was so good during the last quarter of the nineteenth century that they were able to compete with, and out-play most of the Scottish professional teams. It was only in the twentieth century that the club found they were not able to compete with the professional teams around them and eventually entered a downward spiral of decline as a significant force in Scottish football.

As mentioned in the section above, while the typical English game during the 1860s and 1870s was based on individual strength and dribbling, the style adopted by Queen's Park was based on a passing game with less emphasis on individual dribbling. This style was referred to as combination football which Queen's Park gave to England and indirectly to the rest of the world. It was from the mid-1870s and throughout the 1880s that the club really started to develop, and ultimately export this approach. Robinson informs us that Queen's Park never neglected to engage in practise and training. It was during these training sessions that techniques in passing and dribbling were developed (Robinson, 1920).

In fact, Murray goes much further than Robinson by declaring that it was Queen's Park who founded the Scottish game in 1867 and dominated it for the better part of the next 20 years, even after the establishment of Rangers in 1872 and Celtic in 1887 (Murray, 1984). The Queen's Park Football Club in Glasgow is one of the oldest football clubs in the world. From their inception in 1867 until 1875, in all the games Queen's Park played, no team was ever able score a goal against them. The first goal they conceded came in a match with Vale of Leven by one R. Paton just before half-time in a game played in 1875 (Robinson, 1920). What was even more remarkable, given that there were now more teams competing in Scottish football, Queen's

Park never lost a match until 1876 (Robinson, 1920). Queen's Park Football Club was at the zenith of football during the early 1880s (Robinson, 1920).

Such was their dominance in Scottish football that when the first officially recognised international match between England and Scotland occurred on 30 November 1872 at the Hamilton Crescent Partick, all 11 players for Scotland were from the Queen's Park Football Club. The England team, on the other hand, had been drawn from players representing a number of different English clubs. Although this was really a national club against a country, the game ended even with neither side being able to score. In the first match played between these two, the Scottish formation was 2-2-6 while England's team played with a 1-1-8 formation. This demonstrated the different ways in which the two teams approached the game with England placing more emphasis on attacking whereas the Scottish team presented a slightly more balanced approach.

This strong dominance by Queen's Park was not a one-off situation. A few years later when Scotland played England in 1882, seven of the players were from the Queen's Park Club, with one of these being, of course, Andrew Watson who made 36 appearances for this prestigious club between 1880 and 1887. Watson was a key senior player at the club and one of the proponents of this combination-style of football being played in Scotland.

Watson's football ability was often singled out for praise. For example, in the Scottish Cup final in 1881, in which Queen's Park were under a period of sustained pressure against Dumbarton, Watson, along with Rowan the goal keeper and Andrew Holm was described as having the highest ability (Robinson, 1920). These two clubs met again in 1882 in April and Watson was referred to as the player who provided the cross from which Queen's Park scored. Later, both Queen's Park defenders, Andrew Holm and Andrew Watson were praised for their "sure kicking which was the admiration of all" (Robinson, 1920, 118). Had this been a typical game in England, players would have been less inclined to pass the ball, or in this specific case, cross the ball either into space for a forward player to run on to, or as an attempted specific pass to a teammate.

However, Watson was not without fault or blemish. In one game against Partick Thistle in 1885 when both teams were actually playing in Hampden Park, Scotland, in an English Cup fixture (since the very earliest cups games involved teams from both England and Scotland), Watson's performance, along with a few other team mates, was described as "not so good" (Robinson, 1920, 103). It should be noted, however, that Queen's Park won that game 5-1.

In addition to his football ability, Watson had excellent management skills. He served as the secretary of the Queen's Park Club which made him the world's first Black football administrator. This role involved organising match fixtures, handling correspondences, and aspects of the club's finances. He carried out these functions not only while at Queen's Park, but also previously when he played for Parkgrove FC in the 1870s.

Watson also played for the Scottish national team which was, arguably, the best team in the world at that time. Even though his international career was very short and consisted of three appearances between 1881 and 1882, this was particularly momentous. Playing for the Scottish national team was a significant achievement but being made captain of the team speaks volumes of Watson's ability. After having joined Queen's Park in 1880, within a year, Watson's very impressive performances were rewarded when he was appointed captain of the Scottish national team in March 1881. In his first game for Scotland they beat England 6-1 which remains England's heaviest defeat on British soil. He made two other appearances, not as captain, for Scotland. One was against Wales in which Scotland won 5-1 and the third against England in London at the Oval Park where Scotland won 5-1. In all three games the main reason for Scotland's victories was their combination play. Watson was obviously familiar with this style of play and was also very good at it. The fact that Watson a Black man played for the very top club team in Scotland as well as the national team suggests he was an exceptional player. During the 1880s Watson was one of the very best defenders in the country playing for the very best club team in Scotland (if not in Britain) at the time (Queen's Park) as well as the Scottish national team itself. This level of Scottish dominance did not go unnoticed in England and this is why Corinthians of London, which went on to become the very best amateur club in Britain even into the early twentieth century, also sought the services of Watson.

The Corinthians Football Club was established in the season of 1882-1883 by N.L. Jackson. The club selected players only from public school or university educated backgrounds. According to Walvin, the club regularly "inherited skilful players attuned to each other's game and who had the time and money to devote to their game" (Walvin, 1994b, 92). As mentioned above, Watson had been educated at one of the very best secondary schools in London and had gone on to enrol at university. Because of the amount of money left for him after the death of his father, Watson was assured a fairly affluent lifestyle and was therefore an ideal candidate for the Corinthians Football Club, Britain's most elite and exclusive gentlemen's amateur football club. It had a membership of about 50 people and so for Watson to be invited to join them shows he was an extraordinary player and personality.

The club came to prominence in 1884-1885 when they beat Blackburn Rovers 8-1 at a time when Rovers were regarded as the very best team in Britain and had even recently beaten Queen's Park. They played with five forwards who would make long passes into spaces for other players to run into (Mason, 1975). It's interesting to note that two of the members of the Corinthians team in this match had been selected from Queens Park, Dr. John Smith who actually captained the Corinthians team, and Andrew Watson (Robinson, 1920). The main purpose of Corinthians was to showcase the very best amateur footballers in Britain. In 1886 the England team which drew 1-1 with Scotland included two players from Blackburn Rovers and nine from Corinthians. In 1894 when England beat Wales 5-1, the team was composed entirely of players from the Corinthians team (Mason, 1975). In effect, Corinthians had followed the tradition of looking north of the border in order to find the very best talent. Watson would have been eligible to play for this top English amateur side only because of his public school and university education as well as his remarkable football ability as an amateur player.

Through all this, Corinthians remained firmly committed to their amateur status and such was their quality and high standard, they, like Queen's Park in Scotland, were able to seriously challenge the top professional clubs in England until the early part of the twentieth century. In 1904, for example, Corinthians beat the English FA Cup champions Bury 10-3 (Walvin, 1994b). Bury had earlier won the final by a resounding 6-0. The fact that Corinthians could beat them by 10-3 shows their strength and dominance during this period although they were only committed to playing friendly matches because they refused to join the professional league. In 1910 they toured Brazil and the locals were so impressed that Sao Paulo formed a Corinthians of their own in the same year. They remained an amateur club until they were disbanded in 1939.

Conclusion

While many studies on the history of football in Britain have not mentioned or acknowledged his presence or contributions, Guyanese Andrew Watson was a remarkable footballer who played at the very highest level for club and country and was part of the wave of Scottish 'professors' who came south of the border to play for English teams and help to develop the combination style of football. Even though he played as an amateur, Watson's achievements as a footballer could certainly rival, if not surpass, those of Arthur Wharton and Walter Tull. He played for the best national team at the time and also played for the two best amateur clubs in Britain. This would be equivalent to a world class footballer today playing for and captaining the World Cup Champions and also having a very good career with two of the very best European Championship club teams. Despite the fact that Watson played during the period when the amateur game was still the dominant form, for a Black footballer originally from the Caribbean to have played in the very top teams in the world and be part of the Scottish influence which changed the nature of football in England, is highly commendable. The Caribbean has not produced many Watsons in the contemporary period because micro scrimmage is the dominant structure of daily recreational play in communities across the Caribbean. This form of scrimmage which undermines the development of technically proficient footballers is the subject of the next chapter.

Chapter 6

Scrimmage and the Destruction of Football in the Caribbean

Christopher A.D. Charles

Introduction

This chapter takes the controversial view that scrimmage, as it is used in football in the Caribbean, destroys the game. The preoccupation with scrimmage in football in the region without its connection to a systematic structure of coaching does not develop the skills required for players to play effectively on the right sized pitch. Scrimmage football, which is played daily, prevents the development of many professional players and their ability to get contracts to play for the top football clubs in the world. This chapter is not arguing that scrimmage is useless but that it is used inappropriately in the Caribbean. My interest in this issue is a long-standing one which I briefly outline below.

In the early 1980s Tony Talburt (author of Chapter 5) came home to Kingston on a break from his teaching job at Titchfield High School in Port Antonio, Portland, Jamaica. Talburt told me that he had a co-worker, a philosophical Rasta man who was arguing that we shouldn't play scrimmage football because it retards the development of players. Some time later I visited Titchfield High School to get away from the frenzied life of urban Kingston. We played a game of volleyball and then went to play with the Titchfield High School football squad which was training on the field nearby. Shortly after arriving on the field I met this philosophical Rasta man who was the coach of the football team. He divided the 10 members of the squad present into two groups of five and asked Tony and I to join one of the groups. We were told to play a game of six against six on the big field that is normally peopled with 22 players in a game. Tony saw the puzzled look on my face and remarked, "I told you about this man. He doesn't play scrimmage." I had expected the coach to use one half of the big field with two big goals. I fitted in with the squad because

George Thompson had taught me the basics of the game at Kingston College and he had never encouraged micro scrimmage.

The philosophical Rasta man is Don Davis who was the all-American soccer player in the United States in 1975 and was drafted in the North American Soccer League by the New York Cosmos for which he played in the 1976 football season with legendary team mates Pelé of Brazil and Italian goal scorer Giorgio Chinaglia. Don Davis was the conference co-chair of the Inaugural Academic Conference on International Football and raised the issue of the damage to football by the preoccupation with scrimmage in Jamaica at one of the panel sessions. The conversation got testy as the defenders of football scrimmage at the conference challenged Don Davis. Based on discussions I had about scrimmage over the years with colleagues and my discussions with Davis about his ideas, I developed my arguments about how football scrimmage retards the development of high quality footballers.

Don Davis has been a coach in Jamaica for over 30 years. This chapter discusses his ideas. The chapter commences with a brief discussion of scrimmage in various sports followed by a discussion of the Guinness Street Football Challenge in the Caribbean, a four-a-side scrimmage competition and FIFA's futsal and beach football competitions. This discourse is followed by an outline of Don Davis' ideas and an explanation of how scrimmage in football, as used in the Caribbean, destroys the game by preventing the development of technically proficient footballers.

Scrimmage Football in the Caribbean
Scrimmage is an informal game of a sport using smaller units than in the regular game to practise certain skills, tactics and strategies or execute them in competition between units to improve the performance of players. Coaches and trainers in popular sports such as football, ice and field hockey, netball, basketball, cricket, rugby and so on use scrimmage in their practise sessions to develop their players. Scrimmage as outlined in the foregoing is connected to a larger training system and is used to improve the skills and performance of players in standard play. There is a logical progression in the development of technically

proficient footballers and scrimmage is just one of many tools used in this progression (Brobst & Ward, 2002; Smith & Ward, 2006; Croxton & Klonsky, 1982; Hastie & Saunders, 1991).

However, in the case of football in the Caribbean scrimmage is the dominant organisation of recreational play where very small pitches and micro-goals are used preventing players from developing the appropriate technical skills for standard play on a regular sized field or pitch. The disconnection between football scrimmage and the regular game also occurs because scrimmage is not part of a larger developmental football programme. Roland Butcher reminds us that:

> Scrimmage is killing the game in Barbados. This issue is not a Jamaican problem, it is a wide spread [Caribbean] problem. Everywhere you go you see a fellow standing in front of the goal the whole night, and they play for three or four hours and never score a goal. You see the national team play and you don't see one shot in the game" (Butcher, personal communication, 2014).

Butcher's reminder is backed by the evidence provided by the Guinness Street Football Challenge which is a regional scrimmage competition in the Caribbean. The countries that participated in the 2014 football competition were St Kitts and Nevis, Antigua and Barbuda, Dominica, Jamaica, St Lucia, Guyana, Trinidad and Tobago, and St Vincent and the Grenadines. The tournament was organised to allow teams to compete at the parish level or the equivalent local jurisdiction in each country and the winning team from each local jurisdiction competed against each other for the national title. The national title holders from each participating country went to the Regional Guinness Street Football Finals which was held at the Jean Pierre Complex in Trinidad and Tobago from June 6-7, 2014. These teams were deemed the representatives of their countries. The winner of the 2014 tournament was the team representing host country Trinidad and Tobago which defeated the team representing Guyana 2 goals to 1. The winning team received a FIFA accredited introductory advanced level coaching course and US$5,000 (Cowan, 2014; Stamp, 2014).

Given the thesis of this chapter, that scrimmage destroys football in the Caribbean, the pertinent question is why the FIFA futsal and beach football competitions do not destroy football in the countries in which these forms of football are played. Futsal is the indoor football competition with a maximum of five players on each team including the goalkeeper. FIFA has held seven Futsal World Cups to date in 1989, 1992, 1996, 2000, 2004, 2008 and 2012. Brazil has won four of these Futsal World Cup Finals. FIFA has also held the Beach Football World Cup in 2005, 2006, 2007, 2008, 2009, 2011, and 2013. Brazil has also won four of these tournaments. A beach football team also has a maximum of five players inclusive of the goalie (FIFA, 2014b; FIFA, 2014c).

The reasons why futsal and beach football do not destroy football in the countries that play these football forms are that the maximum players allowed is five on a field that is large enough to encourage unencumbered movement and the development of all the footballing skills that are undermined by the confined structure of football scrimmage in the Caribbean. These smaller versions of football use large goals that are smaller than the standard sized goals but much bigger than the micro goals of scrimmage football used in the Caribbean. These forms of football are mini-versions of big field football that fosters the development of the same skills that players learn playing on standard sized fields. For example, these forms of football make use of a goalkeeper which encourages the outfield players to shoot towards the goal. Moreover, in the countries in which futsal and beach football are popular, they are connected to football development programmes that run from childhood to the professional leagues. They are radically different in structure and play from the destructive micro-scrimmage football. Futsal type scrimmage is the exception in the Caribbean rather than the rule.

The Scrimmage Problem in Caribbean Football
There is a lack of philosophy in Caribbean football which reveals shared misunderstandings in the region. The development of the game in the Caribbean doesn't begin at school or in the developmental programmes of the clubs but the scrimmage competitions on the streets or small

pitches in communities. The issue is not merely the small numbers playing scrimmage but the small thinking or lack of appropriate philosophy because of the preoccupation with playing in very small spaces with very small goals (Davis, personal communication, 2014). The national teams of the Caribbean lack the philosophy and foundation that are required, because of scrimmage football. Dennis Howard in chapter seven argues that the absence of a football philosophy in Jamaica has set the national football programme adrift. This problem also exists in the wider Caribbean where football, from the points of view of philosophy, structure, organisation, training and strategy of play, is at a very low level. The problem is made worse by some of the coaches who do not appropriately prepare the players because of their lack of professional training and international experience.

Scrimmage has prevented the development of goalkeepers, strikers that kick the ball well, players with good understanding of space and dimension, players that know how to receive the ball, players that head the ball properly and players that can control the ball on their chests. Football scrimmage also prevents the development of the team approach, and physically fit and technically competent players that can execute corner kicks. I discuss these problems below.

Scrimmage prevents the development of goalkeepers

During the scrimmage game the "goalkeeper" stands in a very small goal for many hours and he or she is not allowed to use his or her hands. This structure turns the goalkeeper into a blocker who uses his head, body and feet (Davis, personal communication, 2014). This structure of play results in fewer goalkeepers in the region developing the requisite skills than would be the case if big field football were the dominant structure of play.

The small spaces used in football scrimmage means that the "goalkeeper" does not have the opportunity to learn several essential skills of good goalkeeping. He or she does not learn how to get the ball out with a goal kick on the standard field of play, how to position and cover the goal and cut down angles to reduce the effectiveness of the strikers or how to throw out or catch the ball and how to dive, and protect himself or herself when going for a ball. The goalkeeper does not learn how to read the game and communicate effectively with defenders and how to construct a defensive wall of players to mitigate the effect of a free kick. Moreover, other problems are highlighted during football scrimmage games because the blockers do not have the opportunity to execute corner kicks and experience penalty kicks. The only role the blocker has in scrimmage football is to prevent the football from entering the very small goal.

Strikers can't shoot effectively

The purpose of football is to score goals. Some forwards suffer from performance anxiety when it comes to scoring goals. Reducing this anxiety requires a specific type of training that strikers do not get enough of because they spend a lot of time playing scrimmage (Davis, 2014). In order to score goals, players have to engage in organised play and learn to develop systems and patterns of play for the top third of the right sized field. The players will control their anxieties and not panic when they are in front of the opponent's goal and score because they are accustomed to playing in front of the big goal. We have to interrogate the scrimmage problem carefully and use the right sized pitches and goals so that players can learn to shoot to the goal effectively. It is unlikely (but not impossible) that how the players strike (kick the ball to the goal with side of their feet) during scrimmage that they will score if they strike this way to a big goal with a goalkeeper.

It is foolhardy to believe that players playing in a confined space and shooting the ball to a very small goal will be able to score in a big goal (Davis, 2014). Scrimmage strikers do not know how to kick the ball properly and they are unlikely to score a goal on the big field because the goalkeepers are able to dive and block shots taken by strikers that kick the ball well much less scrimmage strikers that cannot kick the ball properly. The strikers have to learn to beat the goalkeeper. For example, if the goalkeeper is on the ground the striker has to put the ball over the goalkeeper, this cannot happen in scrimmage.

The small spaces used for scrimmage also do not allow strikers to kick the ball from various angles under pressure from the defenders and they cannot develop the ability to score goals (Davis, personal communication, 2014). They are used to knocking the ball around in small spaces so they tend to keep the ball in their half more than the opponent's half when they are playing on a big field. Good players are socialised to keep the ball in the opponent's half of the big field. The opposite is the case for scrimmage footballers that are not used to going forward as an organised unit and score in the big goal because this is unfamiliar territory. Good coaches that selectively use scrimmage are required to guide the players to develop systemic patterns of play that are appropriate for the top third of the big field. Getting to the last third of the big pitch requires planning.

Players have limited understanding of spaces and dimensions

Football is a game which requires an understanding of spaces and dimensions and the appropriate movements within these spaces (Davis, personal communication, 2014). Players cannot develop this understanding in football scrimmage because they are not able to move adequately in a small space which is clogged. This lack of understanding is evident in how the strikers on Caribbean teams play in that they don't know how to adequately use spaces with the ball or run off the ball. This truncated play is encouraged by some coaches who encourage the use of the very small goals and the very small pitches. There needs to be a fundamental change in Caribbean football philosophy at the community level. The large pitches should be used every day so the players can learn to develop their creative spatial imagination, and become tactically and strategically conscious. Scrimmage doesn't encourage the development of tactical skills because the players just play the ball and they are not required to move a lot to provide support for the team member with the ball.

Football scrimmage does not support players scanning the field and looking from a distance thereby getting a vision of the entire field of play, and knowing what is happening all around so they can make the best strategic passes at the right time (Davis, personal communication, 2014). Players of scrimmage football are not socialised to visually scan for team members and opponents far away. What the players see is what is near their feet and that is about ten metres away because of the scrimmage orientation. There is also no overlapping play in scrimmage so players cannot effectively overlap in a competitive game on a big field. The players in the international leagues that are aired on Caribbean cable television do not play this way and Caribbean players want to be like these international footballers without giving up scrimmage. These international players were not raised on football scrimmage. It is difficult for many people in the Caribbean to see this problem because scrimmage normalises mediocre play.

Players don't know how to receive the ball

At the technical level some Caribbean footballers struggle with the simple technique of receiving the ball. If you do not receive the ball you can't make an impact on the game (Davis, personal communication, 2014). Caribbean players struggle to receive the ball because the everyday scrimmage experience trains them to receive the ball with their backs to the ball. International footballers in contrast receive the ball sideways so that they can see clearly where they want to go with the ball. Many young players in the Caribbean do not know how to view the game because they don't know that is happening behind them. Players turning their backs to the ball are entrenched in Caribbean football culture because of the influence of scrimmage.

Poor heading skills

The packed spaces created by scrimmage football hardly allow players to head the football thereby discouraging the use of the head. It is not that heading does not occur in a football scrimmage game, it just happens infrequently. This infrequency means that many Caribbean players are not good headers of the ball. Many fans will recall instances when local strikers score goals with their heads but are stunned by European professional players' power headers to goals because they are not used to seeing them at home. Caribbean fans are even more amazed at the goals scored from the diving headers of overseas professional footballers.

The infrequency of heading in scrimmage means that some players cannot pass the ball accurately with their heads to a team member. They just head the ball in the direction of their team member. The same problem obtains when a team is under pressure in front of their goal and some players have a difficulty clearing the ball with their heads when the opportunities arise. There are good headers of the ball in the region but they develop this skill from being part of a team with an effective training system which uses scrimmage selectively for training purposes but discourages it as the dominant form of recreational play.

Scrimmage destroys team work

The influence of scrimmage is also evident in the individualism of play on the pitch because each player does his or her own thing playing scrimmage (Davis, 2014). As played in the Caribbean, scrimmage is about passing the opponents. If the players lose the ball they walk towards the ball or stay where they are rather than get behind the ball to help defend against their opponents. This attitude is evident in how some national teams play. The players attack and lose the ball and walk towards the play because they were socialised this way by scrimmage football. These players don't move a lot on the field until they receive the ball in scrimmage so they play for themselves as individuals rather than the team which gets shafted. As Talburt pointed out in chapter five, this goes back to the way the game was first played in Britain where attackers were responsible for dribbling past their opponents rather than passing the ball to their teammates. The scrimmage culture and philosophy creates individuals rather than team mates. Therefore, Caribbean coaches have to adjust their football methodology from the ground up.

Scrimmage football destroys team chemistry because it is about passing opponents in the small spaces which does not encourage passing of the ball (Davis, personal communication, 2014). There is also a hierarchy of talent on the scrimmage pitch with the best players striking up front and the progressively worst players are stationed at the back. What is worse is that the players do not use the opportunity to rotate positions in the small spaces used for football scrimmage. Rotation of positions mostly occurs between players at the front that are tired and the blocker stationed in the goals. The players up front rest as blockers in the very small goals and the original blockers move upfront. More often than not players do not fall behind the ball and cover spaces and mark and tackle opponents when their team is being counter-attacked. The ethos and culture derived from football scrimmage does not encourage team play, as mentioned above, and hence does not encourage team chemistry.

The Jamaican and Trinidad and Tobago football teams that went to the World Cup in 1998 and 2006, respectively, had their technical, positional, social and psychological chemistry interwoven. These teams had their attacking and defensive midfielders, their runners and their playmakers and so on that moved with integrated play. The players complemented each other. It is not surprising that these two national football teams had several players that had been based overseas and were not encumbered by the low skill level, bad attitude and lack of understanding of the game perpetuated by the structure of football scrimmage in the Caribbean.

Lack of physical fitness

Some footballers in the Caribbean are not as physically fit as they should be because they get tired quickly and so they cannot perform effectively. The culture of football scrimmage is that a player only moves when he or she receives the ball and then he or she rests wherever and whenever he or she likes in the small space (Davis, personal communication, 2014). This lack of discipline is entrenched by scrimmage. Players do not run to cover when their teams are under counter attacks during scrimmage, they only rotate positions to rest as blockers in the goal when they are tired. Despite the fact that football scrimmage games may go on for three hours or more, there is not much running because the small space being used does not require constant running backed by physical fitness. Footballers moulded by scrimmage are more likely to be less fit than players moulded on the right sized pitch.

It is not uncommon to hear national footballers in the Caribbean saying to the press that they are not 100 per cent fit and they are working on improving their fitness before the competition. The foreign coaches that come to the Caribbean to coach some of the national teams have to train the national players to get them physically fit by international standards. These national players do not have the discipline to physically condition themselves without their trainers. Celebrated former professional footballer Allan "Skill" Cole of Jamaica noted that some of his fans regularly commented that he was an exceptional footballer so he didn't have to train. Cole argued that this view was stupid because if he wasn't physically fit he could not play consistently well at the national and international levels (Cole, personal communication, 2014).

Poor takers of corner kicks

Corners are not taken in scrimmage given the small size of the pitch. Excellent sport performances cannot be achieved without repetitive action. The set plays of corner kicks on the standard pitch are infrequent because of the influence of scrimmage. The lack of these set plays put Caribbean national teams at a disadvantage as many players, constrained by the structure of frequent scrimmage games, cannot execute in-swinger or out-swinger corner kicks. Very often the player taking the corner kick makes a long run up to kick the ball because she or he is relying on force rather than technique. Sometimes the corner kick taken is too long and goes out for a throw on the other side of the field. A related issue is that throws in scrimmage are one-handed under-arm throws so some players cannot throw the ball properly in a regular game. Caribbean fans from time to time are surprised to see a foul called against a player for throwing the ball incorrectly.

The development of mediocre players

The human congestion which takes place during football scrimmage games in the Caribbean context also does not lead to the development of wingers that can dribble and who can cross the ball accurately, wingbacks and central defenders that know how to defend their goal and provide passes to the players in front of them, and the midfielders that distribute the ball. Scrimmage also retards the development of players that understand the positions and the role of each position on the big field. One example is that defenders that play scrimmage football sometimes do not know how to set the half side trap on the big field and the strikers do not know how to avoid this trap such as running across the face of the goal and the strikers and wingers switching positions and so on. There are also the midfielders whose role on the standard field of play is to service the wingers and the strikers with passes, probe the opposing defence and create paths to the opponents' goal. The Caribbean is not developing good midfielders and other positional players with the requisite skills because of the constraining and confining structures of football scrimmage.

The kind of sophisticated cognition that is required for the various positions on the field do not develop in footballers that are reared on scrimmage (Davis, personal communication, 2014). Football scrimmage doesn't require the strategic thought processes and integrative complexity, where each player understands his or her role and the roles of all the players and conceptually integrates and uses this amalgamation to guide what he or she does with the ball in the service of scoring goals. The biggest thought process in scrimmage play is directed toward dribbling the ball, and shielding the ball from the opponent so this process builds the individual players rather than team members that operate as a strategic and tactical unit.

Conclusion

This chapter has argued that scrimmage football is not intrinsically bad and it is useful for developing certain footballing skills. However, the type of scrimmage played in the Caribbean with very small goals on very small and packed pitches prevents the development of the footballing skills that are necessary for playing at a very high level on the standard pitch. The chapter has argued, therefore, that scrimmage in the Caribbean prevents the development of: (1) goalkeepers; (2) deadly strikers; (3) players with an adequate understanding of the spaces and dimensions of standard sized fields; (4) players that know how to receive the ball; (5) proper heading of the ball; (6) ball control on the chest; (7) the team ethos and chemistry; (8) players that are physically fit; and (9) excellent players. Caribbean coaches need a football philosophy which encourages the playing of futsal type football that are linked to developmental football programmes with the frequent use of standard sized fields to prevent the further destruction of football by the micro scrimmage played in the region. The lack of this football philosophy in Jamaica is the focus of the next chapter.

Chapter 7

From Penna to Schäfer:
In Search of a Jamaican Football Philosophy

Dennis Howard

November 16, 1997 was a very historic day in Jamaican sporting history because on that day the small nation of under three million inhabitants became the first English-speaking Caribbean country to qualify for the greatest sporting event in the world, FIFA World Cup. Thirty teams entered the competition from the CONCACAF confederation to qualify for three spots to the 1998 World Cup in France. After the preliminary rounds, six teams played against each other on a home-and-away basis in the final round. The top three teams from the confederation would qualify. Jamaica was an unlikely candidate for qualification because our record before this was unspectacular while teams such as Mexico, the USA, Costa Rica, Honduras, El Salvador and Canada, the six highest-ranked teams were considered to be among the likely nations to secure one of the three coveted spots. In 1996 Jamaica was ranked a paltry 32 on the FIFA/Coca Cola World ranking of national teams so everyone believed it would be more of the same as far as qualification was concerned.

Captain Horace Burrell, then president of the JFF, was having none of that and he and his team set a plan in motion which would result in this historical moment and achievement for the small country that amazingly continues to punch above its weight class in almost all spheres of modern life.

The JFF hired a Brazilian coach, René Simões as technical director with a team of Jamaican coaches including the stalwart Carl Brown. The federation then went on a recruiting drive to attract players with Jamaican parentage or origin who were playing in the first division and premier leagues in England to add another level of professionalism to the local-based team. Players like Deon Burton, Paul Hall, Fitzroy Simpson and Robbie Earl brought a renewed level of professionalism and work ethic to a local-based team that were playing together for some time including Walter Boyd, Onandi Lowe, Andy Williams,

Theodore Whitmore, Peter Cargill and Warren Barrett. Jere Longman summed up the "fab four", as they were dubbed, addition this way "four players from England who have revived a ragged, deflated team and given it a fighting chance to become the first World Cup qualifier from the Caribbean since Haiti in 1974"(Longman, 1997). The era of the *Reggae Boys* had begun.

The formula paid dividends immediately and national interest in the team began to grow tremendously. The team was unbeaten at home for a very long time due to the support of the twelfth man. The culmination of this process was the qualification of the team at the National Stadium before an estimated 32,000 joyous football fans. Considering that Jamaica did not have even a semi-professional league at the time and no comprehensive infrastructure to support football the appearance in France was a good one. Predictably, Jamaica did not survive the first round but scored first against Croatia which placed third in the competition. Croatia won 3-1. Jamaica's inexperience and lack of organisation was on full display during the 5-0 drubbing by Argentina led by Gabriel Batistuta's hat trick. Jamaica did the unexpected by defeating Japan 2-1 in its final game, with mid fielder Theodore Whitmore finding the net for a brace. Since the success in France in 1998, qualification has, predictably, been elusive for the country and each campaign to qualify since has been plagued with controversy, blunders, mismanagement, ineptness and lack of vision.

A plethora of reasons have been posited as to why we have not qualified since France and many pundits and fans have blamed it on the mismanagement and the lack of vision of the JFF. While there is enough blame to go around on a host of reasons for our under performance, I want to focus on the idea of a Jamaican football philosophy, is there one and if one does not exist why not and are there plans afoot to seriously work on a distinctive Jamaican football philosophy. During Simões' first tenure as technical director he continuously articulated a philosophy but this to my mind was never institutionalised in the footballing system. Simões is reported to have told "players to dance with the ball, to pretend it is their girlfriend at a dance, not to let anyone else steal her away." According to Simões "they play with a very Brazilian philosophy–

confident with the ball, calm and looking for space" (*New Strait Times*, 1998a, 12). "As for the heavies, no one plays hard in Jamaica. I'll have to look to the players from England for that" (*New Strait Times*, 1998b, 12). I will come back to the statement from Coach Simões, but before we interrogate this issue let us focus on what it means to have a football philosophy.

The Oxford Dictionary defines philosophy as "a theory or attitude that acts as a guiding principle for behaviour" however as it relates to a football philosophy, football scholar, Jed Davies suggests:

> A footballing philosophy is defined as: a set of beliefs about how football should be played on the field tactically. Football tactics are assumed to be that of the strategy (ies) employed by a team to defend, attack and everything in between (the two transitions of losing the ball and winning the ball) (Davies, 2013).

A philosophy should be the foundation of how football is played in a particular club team or country. It should be based on the best skills of the team, its cultural specificities, idiosyncrasies, and strategies. In essence, a philosophy provides a blueprint for teams to achieve their goals and encompasses personal and collective beliefs, motivations, collective experience and shared style and identities. This will manifest itself in a particular way and style of playing both on and off the field. It should become a way of being which exemplifies the innate attributes and purpose of the team the ultimate symbol of fraternity and belonging. Former Chelsea manager, Avram Grant, notes, "The days when only tactics were the name of the game have finished – now you need a philosophy" (*Sky Sports*, 2014).

The football philosophy of the major football nations are well documented. The Dutch gave the world *total football (totaalvoetbal)*, this tactical theory revolves around the notion of any outfield player adapting to any role on the field at the appropriate time. Pioneered by Rinus Michels coach for Dutch team Ajax and the national team total football hit the global stage in 1974, which allowed the Dutch team to make the finals of both the 1974 and 1978 World Cup finals. *Total Football* can be described as proactive with players filling positions of other players who are out of position at any given time. So outfield payers can assume roles of attackers, midfielders or defenders throughout the 90 minutes of play on the field. This meant that football players had to be total players who were not one dimensional but highly technical and with physical endurance.

In recent times Spain with its *Tiki-taka* (*tiqui taca*), have seen them dominating world football, winning all the major global titles. *Tiki-taka* is described as a derivative of *total football* adopted in Spain, through the efforts of managers Luis Aragonés and Vicente del Bosque. *Tika - taka* relies on possession football, characterised by short quick passes and constant movement maintaining possession and breaking down opponents in the process. Jed Davies notes that *Tiki-taka* is:

> A conceptual revolution based on the idea that the size of any football field is flexible and can be altered by the team playing on it. In possession, the formation should intend on creating space and therefore making the pitch as big as possible (Davies, 2012).

While tiki-taka has been countered by many teams and imploded at the 2014 World Cup which saw Spain going out in the first round as defending champions, it is hard to discount its effectiveness as a philosophy that guided Spanish clubs like Barcelona and the Spanish national team to major success.

Let us turn briefly to the most dominant football nation Brazil and its philosophy of football. The beautiful game, as football is called in Brazil, is about joy, flair, individual skill, teamwork and the highest technical skill. Educator and former football player José Thadeu Goncalves in *The Principles of Brazilian Soccer*, observes:

> [T]he individual Brazilian player is technically very sound; every player on the field plays comfortably with the ball at his feet. Additionally, he is creative by nature, and while tactically very astute, he also likes to do the simple things with flair. We've all learned to expect the unexpected in Brazil's attacking area of the field (1998, 3).

Ball possession is critical as René Simões noted, the opponent can't score on you if your team has the ball. The ball is in constant movement, "except when crossing, shooting or sometimes when exploiting an opening up front or changing the point of attack from one flank to the other with a single pass" (Goncalves, 1998, 4).

Team unity and communication is a very important part of the Brazilian philosophy, former national coach Carlos Parreira noted, "I didn't have to teach our players how to play soccer, but did have to help them develop as a unit. That is not easy for Brazilian players because they are such individuals" (Goncalves, 1998, 5).

This brief exposé on the football philosophies of Holland, Spain and Brazil, exemplifies the importance of a blueprint to be successful at international football. A football philosophy is a crucial component of any national football programme yet we have seen, in the case of Jamaica and in other Caribbean and African nations, a glaring absence of any efforts to develop a national philosophy unique to the cultural and national specificities of these countries. Avram Grant reminds us that:

> Tactics you can change because players are more intelligent now and you need to think very quickly. Players are more skilful now and you have less time to think. But when you have a philosophy you sign the (right) coach and then you need to stick with him (*Sky Sports*, 2014)

Culture of Adoption vs. Philosophy

Instead of a football philosophy, Jamaica has developed what I call a culture of adoption. A culture of adoption can be described as the consistent importation of personnel, tactics, ideas, structures and mindset from other successful footballing nations and regions imposing them on Jamaican football without taking into consideration if they are cultural fits and will work in Jamaica. This practice is very eclectic, inarticulate and confused and, while bearing some fruits at certain points in our history, has been unsustainable and will not take us forward. Due to this practice of adoption, football has been plagued with certain shortcomings, which I will outline below.

(a) Individual skill

The culture of football starts with the skill of the individual player exemplified in the person of Allan "Skill" Cole, emphasis being placed on the name "Skill". In a team sport Jamaica has unfortunately placed too much reliance on individual players and not on the team as a strong unit. Russell Bell states:

> Jamaica has a history of exceptional talent, with players like Fairy-Boots Alcock, Clarence Passalaigue, Gerry Alexander, Noel Hall, Karl Largie, Lindy Delapenha, Anthony Hill, Syd Bartlett, Allan Cole, Tony Keyes, Trevor Harris, Diego Gordon, Lennie Hyde, Neville Oxford, Bingi Blair, Johnny Barnes, Derrick Dennicer, Dennis "Stylo" Ewbanks, Andy Williams, Ali Rose, Steve Green, Paul Young, Kemal Malcolm, Shamar Shelton, Alan Ottey, and many others (Bell, 2009).

This is a typical description of football in Jamaica, while football historians like Bell can create a laundry list of great individual players there are very few lists of successful teams, notable exceptions include the 1966 national team, the 1966 and 1976 Kingston College triple championship teams and the historic 1998 national team that qualified for the World Cup Finals in France. Developing a team concept I believe is very important to the development of football and the 1998 team exemplifies this principle. They were a real team who played together for an extended period and once the British players were introduced, the local players, well in sync already, adjusted to accommodate the overseas players. The latter also adjusted in what seem to be unimportant but critical ways to play the Jamaican way in terms of camaraderie, goal celebration and that Jamaican swagger.

(b) World Cup focus

Since the Horace Burrell era of football administration Jamaica's goal has been to qualify for each staging of the World Cup without any serious attempt to qualify or be competitive in any other regional or international competition.

This approach has proved to be disastrous and runs counter to any comprehensive development thrust for football. The big footballing nations have used the strategy of competing in the all the junior World Cup competitions, the Olympics and confederation competition. Countries such as Nigeria and Ghana were competitive at the Olympics, which Nigeria won in Atlanta in 1996 beating Mexico, Argentina and Brazil. In 1994 Nigeria qualified for the World Cup in the United States and topped their group in the first round. They have consistently qualified since 1994. This approach allows players to develop and gain international experience and build team chemistry. Most German, Argentine and Brazilian players who compete at the World Cup also competed at the under-17 and 20 World Cup. The practice of assembling players from the United States and Britain with the best local players close to the qualifying period is unworkable in modern football.

(c) Prima donna attitude

The attitude of many of our star players have had a debilitating effect on our overall development. National coaches have been hampered by the indiscipline and attitude of entitlement displayed by many of our top players. While this is not unique to the Jamaican experience (consider players like Eric Cantona, Diego Maradonna, Luis Suarez, Nicolas Anelka and Carlos Tevez), due to the underdeveloped nature of Jamaica football, the super egos as manifested in our star players have had a more deleterious effect than in football cultures where institutional support, consistent developmental paths and economic health are a matter of course. During the campaign to France the conflicts between Walter "Blacker" Boyd and René Simões almost derailed the campaign pitting the coaches and the JFF in a tussle resulting in Boyd, our top player at the time, almost not making the team that went to France. Boyd had to issue a public apology to Simões to be included in the squad to the World Cup. Boyd in his statement noted, "I ask forgiveness and commit to work harder for my own good and that of my family. The last few months have been part of the most difficult period of my life. It has caused me to do a lot of thinking" (Geddes, 1998). Boyd had accused Simões of "playing God" with the national team. He had several lapses in discipline including missing the The RJR National Sportsman and Sportswoman of the Year award ceremony where Deon Burton received the Sportsman of the Year Award.

During the World Cup campaign, Onandi Lowe butted head with René Simões when he was asked to change position during a humiliating 6-0 drubbing in Mexico. Lowe defiantly walked off the field during the game instead of complying with Simões' instructions.

(d) The need for long-term development

Despite its best efforts, the JFF has not been able to articulate a long-term development plan for football. Plans have been too short term and too focused on qualifying for the World Cup. It took a very long time for the organisation to set up any footballing academy and the development of youth and female football is still not at the level that will see exponential growth for football. A major part of any development plan for football requires the proper documentation and recording of the history of football at the local, regional and national levels. This documentation and sensitisation process is completely inadequate, causing a situation, especially among young players, where there is no information or history of the exploits of some of our football heroes.

Football legends such as Lindy Delapenha, Allan "Skill" Cole, Ali McNab, Bunny Goodison, Carl Brown, George Thompson and Walter Boyd are not known by generations of young female and male players. The great teams are even less known and, as stated previously, football in Jamaica privileges individual players and their skill over teamwork which emphasises passing, ball possession and scoring. Tradition is critical to developing the identity, character and culture of any sports. History and dissemination of this history is critical not only to football but also nation building.

We need to encourage patriotism and pride through dissemination of our achievements, small as they are currently, and learn from the Brazilians who are fiercely patriotic to their country. This patriotism leads to a high quality of play when the Brazilians put on their national uniform. In Jamaica, we are just doing a job that we are not passionate about and it shows in the mediocre performance of our national teams.

(e) Looking outward

Don Davis has highlighted the lack of respect that Jamaican coaches experience in the national programme and identifies the need for the development of our home-grown coaches as a major component of any developmental process. He believes that this "...points to an obvious lack of respect and confidence that becomes a sub-textual opening into questions of self-respect, confidence, self-esteem with challenges to the colonial order and manner of leadership" (Davis, 2012). Davis also noted that many home-based coaches have undertaken extensive training. These include Neville Bell, Wendel Downswell, Dean Weatherly, Jerome Waite and Jackie Walters. The JFF's consistent reliance on foreign coaches has resulted in the disrespect perceived by Davis. We can't question the success of foreign coaches to the development of football in Jamaica and many major footballing nations have employed foreign coaches. This points to the fact that nationalism is secondary in world football. However, pundits like Davis point to the lack of a cohesive plan to improve the cadre of Jamaican coaches so that they, too, can offer their skills internationally. This cohesive plan will be possible through their involvement in the various national programmes in a more consistent manner than is the case currently.

(f) The lack of a philosophy

There seems to be no consistent recognition that a philosophy is critical to the development of Jamaican football. Several pundits have made the call but others have noted that it is not a necessity. During his short stint as national coach, John Barnes regularly spoke about the need for a philosophy:

> It is for me to instil in them a footballing philosophy, which will be the feature of Jamaican football and so it's a great opportunity for me to have them for a week and it is going to be worthwhile," (Bailey, 2008).

However, journalist Eldon Tucker believes a Jamaican football philosophy is not attainable:

My attention was also drawn recently to president Boxhill's call for a Jamaican football philosophy or style of play. I think such a philosophy will be hard or even impossible to develop. The Reggae Boys are drawn from diverse leagues in Europe and North America. Some of these players, like those born in England have never played football locally and would find it difficult to fit into a Jamaican system. Rather than focus on a Jamaican style I think our football bosses should put their energies into helping to lift the level of professionalism among local players (Tucker, 2006).

While the tradition of utilising foreign coaches to raise the bar for football has been successful, a defined philosophy which relies on the innate skills and strengths of our home-grown players is lacking. Our athletes are blessed with speed yet we have not developed a game that exploits our pace, which is critical to modern football. This failure to exploit our speed has been evident in the tenure of the foreign coaches from Haitian Antoine Tassy, Brazilian Jorge Penna, Otmar Calder to René Simões and all the other Brazilian imports and now the German Winfried Schäfer. The German has outlined a strategy which places importance on all levels of competition for the national team. In a *Gleaner* article about the Gold Cup Schäfer noted:

It's very important. It's the next step to the World Cup 2018. Money comes when we win... this tournament is very important for our image, for our confidence, and for the Gold Cup. We can learn when we play in the Gold Cup" (Boyd, 2014).

Overseas coaches have made a significant contribution to football with Simões being the most successful. They to some extent all came with a philosophy and varying levels of success. The Brazilians and the JFF attempts to import the Brazilian style failed to understand and successfully come to terms with the psyche, cultural idiosyncrasies and attitude of the home-grown players and totally ignored the perceptions of identity, work ethic, commitment and sense of belonging of the English-born players. In the Brazilian philosophy while individual talent and skill is critical, attributes such as the right attitude, disciplined teamwork, intensive training regimes and nutrition and mental well-being are equally important. Goncalves (1998, 3) reminds us that:

> The Brazilian player works hard and is physically trained in highly scientific, closely monitored methods. This high level of fitness enables him to do the work necessary to supply positive numbers around the ball-both offensively and defensively. Combine fitness with this mix of individual skill, creativity and tactical awareness and you create special players and remarkable teams.

However, there was never a football philosophy that encompassed the best practices of modern international football and one that embraced the innate talent, idiosyncrasies, creativity, joy, culture and swagger of the Jamaican spirit. The football philosophy for a national team is therefore deeply ingrained in the country's history and should reflect the psyche of the entire nation something a foreign coach should adopt while instilling his particular brand of football more and more. International football fans are asking the question: what is your philosophy? Brazil, Germany, England and Italy are all great answers to this question.

Conclusion

Tactical strategies are evolving which makes the beautiful game very exciting and extremely lucrative. Jed Davies summarises the more recent changes which include, more short passing (mixed tempos and complex), and the reliance on a very organised defensive block, reliance on 'team play,' the rising importance of formation and positional balance (tactics), more speed running throughout the game and gaining the advantage in counter attacks, playing with more intensity, more centralised play as a means of scoring or assisting goals, (Davies, 2014) and moving with the ball like one is dancing to reggae and dancehall music.

The Jamaican national team and administration have struggled to develop a clear and identifiable footballing philosophy on the football field and as a result of this have paid the heavy price since 1998. I struggle to see how the national team will be successful in the future without a clear philosophy centred on a total team mantra. The senior national team is known as the Reggae Boys yet the administration seem to be oblivious of the power of reggae and its importance to the Jamaican sense of identity and success. Kwame Dawes in articulating the unique power of the aesthetic of reggae states, "because of its self containedness it defies terms such as 'derivative'" (Dawes, 2004, 18). He continues:

> It is not that reggae does not represent a hybridisation of other kinds of music, but the resultant entity has shown itself to have a coherent character capable of absorbing other influences without losing that coherence. This is, for me the definition of a truly national culture (Dawes, 2004, 18-19).

Dawes is on to something crucial which explains the special quality of an important component of our culture.

The key to future success is the development of a football philosophy steeped in our shared Jamaicaness no matter the origin of the individual. The culture of adoption must be rooted out and replaced with a truly Jamaican philosophy, which while absorbing the best international practices does not lose its coherence and unique identity. However, the change is not sustainable if the change is not a holistic and comprehensive one. The Jamaican philosophy and developmental plans must permeate all levels of football. That means at the primary and high school levels and especially in the National Premiere League. A paradigm shift in the overall developmental thrust of football has to be undertaken and central to this is the acceptance of developing a philosophical approach to playing the game. In describing the English Premiere League Jed Davies reminds us that:

> Like no other, the English Premier League has grown into the most tactically diverse league; a league where the full

spectrum of philosophies and playing styles match wits and bring about the unpredictability of results. While football will continue to evolve world-wide, the English Premier League has developed a sense of individuality from team to team; a real sense of philosophical belief specific to each club (Davies, 2014).

Similar sentiments hold true for most of the top leagues in the world including Serie A, Bundesliga, Eredivisie, J League and La Liga. We can safely say, the era of the skilful individual player who carries a team on his or her back all the time is over. The use of technology will have to take centre stage, as was evident with Germany's success in Brazil. Nicolas Jungkind, SAP's head of soccer sponsorships, noted that speed was an important focus for the German team at the 2014 World Cup in Brazil. Jungkind noted that with technology the coaching team was able to analyse stats about average possession time and reduce it from 3.4 seconds to about 1.1 seconds, the technology was able to identify and visualise the change and show it to coaches, players and scouts. Jungkind observed, "That then goes into the game philosophy of the German team. What is apparent is the aggressive style Germany plays" (Norton, 2014). Teams are very organised around solid philosophical and tactical approaches to modern football. You only have to look at the success of fellow CONCACAF teams such as Mexico and Costa Rica in Brazil in 2014 to understand that the culture of adoption is unworkable and will not bring the success Jamaica has been hoping for which is qualifying repeatedly for the World Cup. Jamaica's only appearance at the World Cup is discussed in the next chapter.

Chapter 8

Reggae Boys:
Putting Jamaica on the World Football Map

Hilary Robertson-Hickling

Introduction

The title of this chapter comes from Robbie Earle, one of the first Reggae Boys to score a goal at the 1998 FIFA World Cup in Jamaica's match against Croatia. He was one of the Boys that was born in England of Jamaican parents and who came from the Jamaican Diaspora half of the team. The other half of the team was made up of local Jamaicans. Earle wrote in *The Gleaner* of Monday, October 21, 2013, "I think the goal helped to put Jamaican football on the world map and that the Reggae Boys are now being taken more seriously." Earle's comment is even more significant when viewed alongside the following statement made in the Introduction of the book *Jamaica's Reggae Boys*, "Now out of the Caribbean, a team from an island known mainly for its music, its beaches, a failing economy and a terrifying crime rate, had stepped onto a world stage, one of the players barely 19, to attest to the raw talent and indomitable will of the Jamaican people" (Bailey & Muller, 1998, 7).

I became interested in the significance of a sport team to national identity when I lived in New Zealand in 1994 and learned about the national rugby union team the All Blacks. The team's identity and performance combined a number of elements of the embodiment of masculinity, the *Haka* a Maori war dance which is a ritual which starts every game, fearless gamesmanship and sleek well-tuned bodies. The team combined Maori and European elements and was famous around the world for its skill and commitment to the game of rugby.

Soon, I would spend my Saturday afternoons watching the games played across the country and internationally. Much to my own amazement I would learn such names as Sean Fitzpatrick, the captain, and Tuigamala. Hence, I became hooked on rugby and on New Zealand.

Later when I lived in England between 1997 and 2000 I supported the New Zealand team when it played in the Rugby World Cup in the UK. This explains how a Jamaican woman who knew little about rugby began to think and reflect about the importance of sport to national identity. I had also read the work of James (1993) *Beyond a Boundary* about the importance of cricket to West Indian identity during the colonial and post-colonial periods.

While I lived in New Zealand, the impetus that was to grow into what was to be Jamaica's World Cup campaign the "Road to France" was taking shape. In the year 1994 the JFF elected Horace Burrell as president. In following the advice of CONCACAF head the controversial Trinidadian Jack Warner, Captain Burrell devised a plan to recruit a good foreign coach and to raise the considerable sponsorship which would be required.

There were many sceptics but Horace Burrell a retired army officer turned successful businessman used all of his considerable skills to persuade, cajole and otherwise make the impossible possible. As the team's performance improved Captain Burrell set to work in the private sector and by 1997 the Road to France had 86 sponsors. One feat that Burrell accomplished was the recruitment of René Simões a Brazilian who was recommended by the Brazilians. Simões led the Jamaican team to qualify and was assisted by successful former Jamaican national player turned coach, Carl Brown. This chapter explores the development of the team from its conception to the point of its qualification at the World Cup Football in 1998 using Tuckman's model.

Tuckman's Model

The important task at hand was how to assess the development of the 1998 World Cup Team, its successes and failures as well as other lessons which we can learn from the experience. Tuckman's model will be used to explain the development of the team from its formation to its adjournment. The model will be applied to data gleaned from secondary sources. The chapter also looks at how the 1998 World Cup Campaign highlights Diaspora and identity and finally examines the lessons which can be learned from the qualification of Jamaica's national football team to the World Cup.

Tuckman's short article was published in 1965, "Development sequence in small groups". It has been the most influential model of group development process, certainly in terms of texts aimed at practitioners. The initial four-stage model evolved out of Tuckman's observation of group behaviour in a variety of settings and his encounter with the literature. Many have adopted a version of Tuckman's model – *forming, storming, norming and performing*. Tuckman later added a fifth stage *adjourning* (Tuckman & Jensen, 1977).

Forming

Groups initially concern themselves with orientation accomplished through testing. Such testing serves to identify the boundaries of both interpersonal and task behaviours. Coincident with testing in the interpersonal realm is the establishment of dependency relationships with leaders, other groups or pre-existing standards. It may be said that orientation, testing and dependence constitute the group process of *forming* (Tuckman & Jensen, 1977).

In the case of the Reggae Boys there were home-grown players and those born of Jamaican parents in the Diaspora from which the team could be selected. Each player was called up to play for their country and the training sessions served as the testing for the World Cup. To move from a group to a team the Reggae Boys shared a common goal of qualifying for the World Cup and doing well at the tournament so there developed a dependency relationship as each player had to perform in his role and position to create an effective team. There was the perception that the foreigners were seen as the better players and were favoured during forming. Despite the foreign versus local schism, the Jamaican national identity and the love for the game and the opportunity to represent Jamaica at the World Cup in France held the team together.

Storming

The second stage is characterised by conflict and polarisation around interpersonal issues, with concomitant emotional responding in the task sphere. These behaviours serve as resistance to group influence and task requirements and may be labelled as *storming* (Tuckman

151

and Jensen, 1977). There was considerable conflict about many issues including the selection of the team from the Jamaican Diaspora and at home. There was a need for a delicate balance between both groups. There was the need to provide opportunities for those in the country, many of whom were from poor backgrounds who would greatly benefit economically and professionally and those with international experience. The World Cup team required a careful balance for high level performance (Tuckman & Jensen, 1977).

The team included, Paul Hall, Robbie Earle, Deon Burton, and Fitzroy Simpson who were based in Britain, Ricardo Gardener, Peter Cargill, Warren Barrett, Gregory Messam, Walter Boyd and Theodore Whitmore, Fabian Davis, Dean Sewell, Linval Dixon and Onandi Lowe among others who were based in Jamaica.

There was tension and sometimes animosity between the British players and the locally-based players. This affected performance. In one game, the burly forward Lowe powered his way into the 18 yards box from the right wing, but the goal keeper had the advantage by covering the angle to the near post and the far post so it was difficult if not impossible for Lowe to score. If Lowe kicked the ball the goalkeeper would just block it with his body and the ball would go for a corner. The text book play was for Lowe to pass the ball to his teammate Burton at the far post who was yelling for the ball. Alas, Burton was British so Lowe rather than pass the ball to Burton kicked the ball and the goalkeeper blocked it with his body and the ball went for a corner to the Jamaican team. Lowe, after he made the foolish shot, stood with his hands akimbo wondering why the ball didn't pass the goalkeeper. He didn't score the goal because he didn't want to pass the ball to the British member of the team whom he hated. This incident in the storming period prevented Jamaica from scoring but the team survived the period.

Norming

Resistance is overcome in the third stage in which in-group feeling and cohesiveness develop, new standards evolve, and new roles are adopted. In the task realm intimate, personal opinions are expressed. Thus we are at the stage of *norming* (Tuckman & Jensen, 1977).

So what are the norms that we have? What kind of behaviours are we going to allow? What is right and what is wrong? And, who is going to be punished and who is not going to be punished. We know that in Jamaica there is a fairly high level of tolerance for transgression, and so people say give the bad boy a chance. I shouldn't be calling the person a bad boy but this was someone who was not, in fact, conforming to conventions of acceptable behaviour. So that was an issue that the team had to go through on several occasions. There was resistance to change. Some of the Jamaican players were never exposed to professional values in their football careers before making the Reggae Boys team. Some of the local players had to learn how to behave as part of a national team playing at the World Cup.

The related issue was how team members were going to function in Jamaica and internationally without the required discipline. Some of the players were not very coachable and disciplined so there was the need to develop appropriate behavioural norms as in the case of players such as Onandi Lowe and Walter Boyd who were discussed in the previous chapter. These were talented but indisciplined players that Coach Simões had to punish, which sometimes angered the Jamaican public. It is alleged that Boyd didn't like to attend training sessions but he expected to do well for his country at the World Cup. The indiscipline on the team was also seen in a match against Mexico at the Azteca where Coach Simões asked Lowe to play as a central defender rather than as a centre forward and Lowe left the pitch in anger.

Performing

Finally, the group attains the fourth and final stage in which the interpersonal structure becomes the tool of task activities. Roles become flexible and functional, and group energy is channelled to the task. Structural issues have been resolved, and structure can now become supportive of task performance. This stage can be labelled as *performing* (Tuckman & Jensen, 1977).

The process which saw the Reggae Boys succeeding at qualification was the ultimate stage in performance. This feat went beyond the wildest dreams of people inside of and outside of Jamaica. By this time they had passed through the uncertainty of forming, the conflicts and tensions between local and overseas players during storming and were now at the stage of performing. One of their highest performances just before the World Cup was drawing a match with Brazil in the COPA America Cup. During the World Cup finals in France in 1998 they won 2-1 against Japan and lost 5-0 against Argentina and 3-1 against Croatia. The Reggae Boys scored three World Cup goals, an outstanding achievement for a team from a developing country which had qualified for the World Cup finals for the first time.

Adjourning

"*Adjourning* involves dissolution. It entails the termination of roles, the completion of tasks and reduction of dependency" (Forsyth, 1990, 77). Since the team qualified in 1998 there has been a process which has resulted in an effort to field a team for all of the subsequent World Cups. Jamaica has not qualified for the tournament since 1998 because the proper structures, programmes and philosophy were not in place when the roles of the players were terminated and their tasks at the World Cup were completed and the team adjourned. It should be noted that Jamaica's qualification for the 1998 World Cup galvanised not only Jamaicans at home but also those living overseas and Caribbean nationals around the world.

Identity in the Diaspora

The Reggae Boys played a series of friendly games in England and elsewhere in preparation for the World Cup. These matches were always well attended by several generations of Jamaicans and other Caribbean nationals. There was the signature smoke from the many marijuana cigarettes that is typical of football games attended by Jamaicans. The Diaspora Jamaicans not only attended games played by the Reggae Boys they closely followed the team's qualification journey to the World Cup made easy by the technology of globalisation (Back, Crabbe & Solomos, 1998; Geddes, 1998).

Fans of the Jamaican team watched the qualification matches at home and in taverns. The most momentous of these matches was the

Jamaican team's 0-0 draw with Mexico in Kingston at the National Stadium (locally called the office) which qualified the team for the 1998 World Cup on November, 16, 1997. This crucial victory resonated with the Jamaican community in particular and the Black community in general in Britain. Black football fans expressed their identity and connections with Jamaica through the qualification matches (Back, Crabbe & Solomos, 1998; Glaser, 2007).

Blacks who congregated to watch the friendly games in stadia and the qualifying matches in taverns cheered the Jamaican team and created a carnival-like atmosphere with reggae and calypso music blaring and Jamaican and other Caribbean food being sold. The fans of the Jamaican football team who came from several generations in Britain saw the qualification to the World Cup as a colossal achievement because a small developing country achieved a national milestone which inspired its citizens. There were pre-games concerts for the friendly games where football and Caribbean music were integrated because reggae artistes like Jimmy Cliff and Dennis Brown performed at these concerts in England. Dancehall icons like Yellow Man, Bounty Killer and Beenie Man and other artistes were among the fans that supported the national team when it played at the National Stadium in Kingston. These events in Jamaica and the Diaspora were not without the dancehall sound systems. The Jamaican football fans in England travelled safely and peacefully to games challenging the stereotype of the wild and violent Jamaicans (Back, Crabbe & Solomos, 1998).

There were anti-racist campaigns in England to get Blacks to attend football games but this campaign was not as effective as the pull of the Reggae Boys qualification for the World Cup. The feat of the Reggae Boys brought the Diaspora together. There was a massive show of support for the Jamaican football team. Jamaicans living in Miami, Atlanta, Toronto, London, New York and Birmingham and so on, flocked Paris in the national colours. The world-renowned dancehall sound system, the Immortal Stone Love was in attendance so football fans rocked to the reggae and dancehall music in Paris. A strong national identity and pride were expressed with deep affection for the Reggae Boys team by Jamaicans at home and abroad. The Reggae Boys finished 22nd in the World Cup out of 32 teams (Back, Crabbe & Solomos, 1998; Geddes,

1999). There are several instructive lessons that arise from the Reggae Boys' participation in the 1998 World Cup.

Lessons from the Road to France

Selection of players

One of the issues I think we have to look at is the selection of the best players from at home or in the Diaspora. And, of course, we know that Robbie Earle has Jamaican parents, and was born in Britain and grew up there, and he has been very articulate about the need for the balance between home-grown and foreign-grown players. I think that one of the most important lessons is that we don't have to have tension between the two groups of players because both groups are Jamaicans. We have to work out the selection criteria to identify the best players to compete on the world stage.

Leadership

So, we realise that leadership is a critical part of this idea of how to achieve something like the qualification of a nation for the World Cup. Horace Burrell's own leadership has been controversial but successful and there have been discussions about the strengths and weaknesses of the JFF. Leadership and the organisations in which leadership is displayed are critical to the success of new ideas and innovations. There must be team leadership which draws on the leadership talent pool rather than the "one don' leadership" which is authoritarian, obstructionist and isolates talent. The importance of sport for national development is still a matter which is in the process of being addressed in Jamaica, and for which the local and international private and public support is necessary for international success. And so there must be further discussion about how important is the national project of football to Jamaica.

The importance of Diaspora to national development

The Diaspora rallied around the team whenever it played overseas where Jamaicans lived. These Jamaicans celebrated Jamaican food, music and other cultural products and provided a ready market for popular music artistes and other cultural performers. The Jamaicans in the Diaspora have a lot to offer the country in terms of investments and competencies in which the country is short. The government should harness the love Jamaicans overseas have for their country in the service of national development. It is not enough to have Diaspora meetings and create Diaspora advisory boards. We need strategic and effective partnerships between Jamaicans at home and abroad to achieve development. We should also be cognisant of the unifying power of sports because the Reggae Boys qualification for the 1998 World Cup was partly credited for the reduction of political violence in the 1997 General Election.

Crucial link between music and sport
Sport, like music, is a very important part of our cultural industries. Music and sport are intertwined as was evident in the dancehall atmosphere at the National Stadium when the national team was playing and the stage shows and dances kept by the Diaspora when the Reggae Boys were playing overseas. We should harness the twin power of music and sport for marketing of Jamaican goods and services in the global marketplace and for pedagogy with young people who are some of the most energetic and loyal supporters of sports and music. We should also encourage our footballers to move with the ball on the field of play as if they were dancing to reggae and/or dancehall music.

Need for sustained presence in international football
The absence of a long-term development plan for football backed by the government and the private sector that goes beyond qualifying for a World Cup is why Jamaica has not qualified for a World Cup final since 1998. This long-term plan requires the appropriate vision, resources, football programmes at all levels and the requisite pool of talent to succeed. This plan must also be a part of the plan for national development.

Caribbean regionalism
The support for the Jamaican football team abroad also came from Caribbean nationals in the region and the Diaspora. Caribbean nationals were also ecstatic about Jamaica's qualification. They were

also in attendance at the football games when the Reggae Boys were in town and attended the pre-match concerts and after match dances. Similarly, Jamaicans and other Caribbean nationals were very supportive of the Trinidad and Tobago team which qualified for the 2006 World Cup. This support from Caribbean nationals is a statement to Caribbean leaders that regionalism in the Caribbean and the Diaspora is alive and well and there is a "we thing" among Caribbean nationals at home and abroad.

Conclusion

The Reggae Boys put Jamaica on the global football map. In support of this we need to document our football experiences in books and film in the same way that James's *Beyond a Boundary* explored cricket and identity, and the recent film *Fire in Babylon* about the West Indies cricket team deepens our understanding of the issues raised by James. There has been some literary documentation such as Earl Bailey and Nazma Muller's book, *Jamaica Reggae Boys World Cup,* an incredible article from Germany by Werner Krauss, *Football Nation and Identity* and so on. Jamaica has benefited considerably from this experience of qualification and we need to dissect it more carefully, we need to be writing more about it and the experiences of the other Caribbean nations that qualified for the World Cup such as Cuba, Haiti and Trinidad and Tobago. We need to have ongoing conversations about how the football impacts Jamaica's national identity, in particular, and Caribbean identity in general. As a nation, how do we work in teams, what is the balance between our collective and our individual identities? Teamwork in the workplace, on the football field, or elsewhere in national life is something that we have to improve.

Jamaica's World Cup qualification in 1998 has meant that a lot of the naysayers and the people that believed that it wouldn't happen, that it was a stupid idea, realised that for the first time people said yes we could, it was possible for us to qualify. At the end of this cycle, the discussion came around to what we would have to do to make it possible to qualify repeatedly.

Can our Caribbean teams cope with the high level of performance of international football? What are some of the lessons that we have learnt from the World Cup qualifications of Cuba, Haiti, Jamaica and Trinidad and Tobago? In the case of Jamaica, we are going to have to find a way to achieve a balance between the home-grown and the foreign-based players. We know that we also need to have transformational leadership in football. There is need for financial resources in this cash-strapped, developing country and the appropriate infrastructure for our footballers to do well. We need to start seeing football as a global business where each Caribbean country, working alone and together, builds the kinds of developmental football programmes that are professional and marketable so that Caribbean teams qualify for every World Cup. One important issue long ignored but important for future World Cup qualification is the use of psychiatrists and psychologists to teach mental skills to enhance the performance of footballers. The next chapter addresses this issue.

Chapter 9

On the Role of Psychiatry in Football

Frederick W. Hickling

Many millions of adults and children from every country watch and play the beautiful game of football. The game is about players and about spectators because football is big business which requires great effort, tension, will and concentration. It is a contest demanding temperance, bravery, skill and self-control that brings out the very best, and sometimes the very worst of people, teams and nations. In this chapter I am going to focus on the *role of psychiatry in football*, which is a small aspect of the psychology of this beautiful game. The British Broadcasting Corporation (BBC) reported that for the World Cup 2014, the football coach for England, Roy Hodgson, recruited a psychiatrist Dr. Steve Peters to be the team psychiatrist (BBC, 2014). Of course the question is, why are psychiatrists needed in football teams? Does the Jamaican football team need a psychiatrist? Hopefully my discussion will address this question, and reveal my affirmative answer. Jamaicans fear psychiatrists and psychologists, especially in national sporting teams.

There is no doubt that this fear is related to the stigma associated with mental disorders. Research and study reveal that there are two types of stigma. The first major realisation of stigma originates from the institutionalisation of people in lunatic asylums like the Bellevue Psychiatric Hospital. This profound and fundamental actualisation is called structural stigma. My own research in Jamaica has revealed that as one moves the practice of psychiatry out of and away from the hospital, people's anxieties and fears of mental disorders diminish dramatically. Today in Jamaica, most psychiatry is practised in the community, and many Jamaicans have come to realise that one does not have to come into a mental hospital to be treated by a psychiatrist. Most of the psychiatrists that we are now training in this country are being educated to practise in the community, so that they treat people in the free, open and unrestricted social space of the society where we live and among our families where we conduct our lives. Some phenomenal and revolutionary treatments with persons who have severe mental disorders have been carried out in the Jamaican community over the past 50 years. Thus many Jamaicans have begun to lose their fears and anxieties about people with mental disorders, and often become the caregivers of those with mental disorders in their social spaces. They are helping to provide therapy for those who have severe mental disorders.

The other kind of stigma is based on individual internal perceptions, and in our culture stigma is rooted in the business of obeah and spiritualism. These fears stem from beliefs about mental disorders by some, which include spirit possession, witchcraft, divine retribution and capture of the soul by the spirit. Such fears are related to the perceptions about mental disorders such as anxiety, depression, bipolar disorder, obsessive-compulsive disorder, personality disorder and schizophrenia. We colloquially call persons with these conditions *the insane, the junkie, alcoholic, the freak, and the crack head.* These are the 'street' names that we associate with mental disorders. Conventionally, we are challenged to understand the problems inside our heads and connect the study of the mind and brain in our lives and in our society. Today we are dared by some to talk about *brain disease* instead of talking about insanity and mental disorders. But for many, this synonym really doesn't help, and does not reduce the stigma it generates.

Professional experience demands that study and research must always start with clinical observation that dictate the direction of qualitative study leading subsequently to the quantitative study, before we can proceed to the causative analysis and understanding of the problem. This chapter on psychiatry in football in Jamaica is based on my own clinical experience of 45 years in Jamaica, and addresses aspects of mental illness and sport, mental skills training, management and mental health, and of the understanding of how to progress a team from the corner league to the World Cup. I will present four case studies from my clinical experience that will illustrate some problems that demonstrate the relationship between psychiatry and football in Jamaica. Looking at the patterns of mental illness in Jamaica, in the early twenty-first century, about 70 per cent of people in Jamaica will have suffered from some form of mental disorder some time in their life. This reality is frightening because it means that most people will have a mental disorder at some time.

Case Study 1: Psychiatric Focus on the Individual

A 40-year-old Jamaican man consulted me at my office at Connolley House in Kingston. He was a well-known professional footballer in the Jamaican Premier League. When he came to see me he was experiencing the symptoms of nervousness, depression, anxiety, and overwhelming feelings of sadness and worry. He had not fully realised that as men in our culture get older, things happen to our bodies. The client had put on weight and was beginning to develop a paunch, and all of these issues were worrying him. He was recognising that, in fact, he was not physically equipped for active professional football and he couldn't cope with the very hard-nosed discipline that was his daily life. This footballer was also thinking about how he was going to live with advancing age; whether he had put enough money aside for his retirement; how he would handle the problems of getting old in football. He went through all the stages of psychological well-being related to developing insight, starting with normal functioning, and progressing to shock and denial, and anger, feelings of depression and detachment from his present condition, with the resulting dialogue, bargaining, and acceptance of the problem, and then the return to meaningful life. During treatment he went through all of the psychological phases working with me from denial of the reality of the problem, through a phase of anger and then through a phase of depression until, finally, he accepted the reality of his condition. Initially, however, he demanded that I find a way to fix his problem instantly as he had an important football match to play the following week. In the spirit of compromise I met him at the football stadium on the evening of the match, and in the interval I took him through a series of relaxation exercises and induced him into a light hypnotic state. At the beginning of the second half of the football match he went from the treatment table onto the field for his team and within one minute he scored a sensational goal. He then came off the field in glory and took no further part in the match. Satisfied with this initial intervention he then had to confront his retirement problems following the football match. We had to find a solution, and work out how he was going to spend his time in retirement after football.

This first case study illustrates the significant role of psychiatry for individual players in football, and indeed in all sports. The players of all sporting activities, whether individual or team sport are all vulnerable to mental disorders at different periods of their lives. The psychiatrist must be able to provide the correct diagnosis and treatment of whatever the nature of the mental disorders in footballers might be and must be accessible to players. The society and the team must facilitate access to these practitioners, and the negation of stigma has to be a priority in the sport. Psychiatrists can play a significant role in the rehabilitation of players after physical illness especially football injury. Retirement planning for professional footballers must be a key element in the delivery of mental health in all sport but especially in the demanding, high-prized team game of football. The management of super talented players is especially relevant in this regard. The infamous biting incident at the 2014 World Cup with Luis Suarez, the Uruguayan striker banned for four months for biting the Italian defender Giorgio Chiellini, illustrates the critical role for psychiatry in the beautiful game. Suarez's defensive denial simply serves to underscore the psychopathology. "After the impact ... I lost my balance, making my body unstable and falling on top of my opponent," Suarez wrote in a letter, dated June 25. "At that moment I hit my face against the player, leaving a small bruise on my cheek and a strong pain in my teeth" (Freidman, 2014). This was the third biting scandal in the career of Luis Suarez (Mullock, 2014). He was banned from professional soccer for four months by FIFA following the incident.

Case Study 2: Psychiatric Focus on the Team

Jamaican schoolboy football has been organised into an elaborate competition that pits football teams from urban and rural secondary schools against each other. This second case study relates to the Jamaican Inter Secondary Schools Sports Association football competition the Manning Cup. This popular annual schoolboy competition among high school under-19 boys' teams is followed avidly by supporters of the schools and of the sport in the parishes of Kingston and Saint Andrew and Saint Catherine. Originating in 1909, it is a precursor to the adult semi-professional football competition – The National Premier League – in the country, which provides an opportunity for semi-professional employment for some of Jamaica's talented young players. The competition often tends to pit the performance of the more recently created urban schools against the long-established urban schools.

The coach of one of these young schools came to see me at my professional office and reported that he had dominion over a Manning Cup team of adolescent boys from his school. He indicated that the team consisted of some extremely talented players, some even performing at 'stellar' quality levels. However, he continued, the team had lost every match in the Manning Cup fixture for that season, and that he was seeking my professional help in resolving the difficulties that they were having and that he was experiencing with them. The young players, he reported, were very individualistic, played very selfish football, and did not relate to leadership or coaching in the team. If one player was having a conflict with another, they would not pass the ball to each other. The narcissistic schoolboy footballers refused to acknowledge the team captain, and would often refuse to take instructions from the coaching staff. There was a sense of irritation, annoyance and distrust within the team, and frustration at their lack of successful performance.

I invited the 22 members of the team and their coaches to participate in a group therapy activity. We sat together in a circle at my office, Connolley House, in Kingston. I invited each participant to say a few brief words about himself and his upbringing, and the role that he played in the team. It was a profoundly cathartic experience – the 'letting go' of emotional tension in the room was palpable. Every single boy in the room reported their social origin from the inner city garrison communities of Kingston (Charles, 2002; Charles, 2004; Charles & Beckford, 2012), and of being *fatherless in a fractured social family* relationship. That brief introduction, within a few minutes almost every boy in the room was weeping! Every single adolescent boy and some of their coaches, on that schoolboy

Manning Cup football team, weeping, tears of frustration, anger and rage of the fact that not one had a father living at home with them. Their minds seemed shattered like a broken mirror; they were experiencing unforgiving and inconsolable grief. I had to handle this extraordinary phenomenological experience by generating a deeply reflective discussion about absent fathers, attachment disorders, abnormal power management and authority relationships, and the genesis of narcissistic personality disorders. Both coaches and the players developed overwhelming new *insights* about their behaviour on the playing field and resolved openly at that meeting to change their behaviour and their style of relating to authority issues in their lives and in their football game.

Attachment issues

The schoolboy footballers in that group psychotherapeutic meeting were expressing rage towards these absent fathers in their life. And whatever love they had in their lives had soured into hate. They were grieving the loss of someone they wanted and needed to love. Grief is not a disorder; it's not a disease or a sign of weakness. It is an emotional, physical and spiritual necessity, and it's the price we pay for love. The only cure for grief is grieving. The adolescent boys on that team were experiencing unforgiving and inconsolable grief (Stolorov, 2013). Anybody who works with people's emotions in Jamaica, especially with young men, will acknowledge that this is something that we see often in this country that is riddled with conflict and trauma. Those of us who do this work recognise this problem in our womenfolk too. Children often report to me that their father who ignored them when they were children, would be the same person to boast of their children's successes as soon as they started showing good or excellent performance. We have to understand that the critical periods of childhood development is in the first thousand days of life (Gillespie, Haddad, Mannar, Menon & Nisbett, 2012). This is the most important period of human development, and that's where mental disorder or wellness starts. It is during this period where a vital process of emotional development begins. This vital process is called *attachment* which is the enduring bonds that hold two or more

166

persons together where regular contact is desired and distress occurs when there is separation (Ainsworth & Bowlby, 1965).

A study of nutritionally-stunted Jamaican toddlers exposed to one-hour-weekly visits from Jamaican community health workers over a two-year period teaching parenting skills and encouraging mothers to interact and play with their children in particular ways revealed that these interventions would develop their children's cognitive and personality skills (Walker, Wachs, Gardner, Lozo, Wasserman, Pollitt & Carter, 2007). The Jamaican stimulation intervention proved to have large impacts on cognitive development in these children 20 years later (Walker, Chang, Vera-Hernandez & Grantham-McGregor, 2011). Stimulation of nutritionally-stunted children during the first 1000 days of life increased the average earnings of these participants by 42 per cent when scholars from the National Bureau of Economic Research in Cambridge, Massachusetts and from the UWI followed them up 2 decades later (Gertler, Heckman, Pinto, Zanolini, Vermeersch, Walker, Chang & Grantham-McGregor, 2013). Twenty years later, the earnings of the stunted children who had received stimulation during infancy in the treatment group had caught up to the earnings of a matched non-stunted infant comparison group. These findings indicated that psychosocial stimulation early in childhood in disadvantaged settings had substantial effects on personal economic growth and the labour market outcomes and thus proved that this early intervention would reduce later life inequality.

When children grow with abuse, when their emotional and physical needs are not met in these first thousand days, they may grow into mistrustful and detached adults and they get different types of *attachment disorders* which will produce abnormal behaviour, which psychological professionals will have to treat in adult life. The National Centre for Fathering in the United States has recently reported that more than 24 million children live in a home in that country without the physical presence of a father. The report indicates that millions have dads who are physically present, but emotionally absent. It is the Black population in the United States (US) which has the largest number of absent fathers (more than 50%, between 2000 and 2010). That statistic is nearly twice as much as for Hispanics, and nearly three times as much as Whites (US Census Bureau, 2012). Fatherlessness is not seen as a public health issue like community violence so it is not given a lot of public attention. The accurate epidemiological data for Jamaica is not yet available. Jamaican anthropologist Herbert Gayle reports that:

> Father presence in the home of the child is growing dramatically (0% in 1838, 15-18% prior to our first election says material I found at the Colonial Office, 37% in 2001 and 42% now; mother absence is increasing noticeably (down from 92% in the 1980s to 84% in 2011. So today 42% of children have their fathers in their homes and 70% have direct access - 9-10% of children do not know their fathers (Gayle, personal communication, June 2014; Hodges, 2014,).

Gayle also reveals that only three per cent of the adolescent boys that he has surveyed in inner city Jamaica identified his father as being the person he spends the majority of his time with and who is, therefore, his primary source of influence (Gayle, personal communication, 2014; Williams-Raynor, 2011).

Narcissism

The team members who were in my office had no respect for the captain of the team and little respect for the coach, and would often question their authority. This group was a football team of *narcissists*. Narcissism is the pursuit of gratification from vanity or egotistic admiration of one's own physical or mental attributes that derive from arrogant pride. In Greek mythology, Narcissus was a hunter renowned for his beauty. Nemesis was a beautiful woman who lured Narcissus to a pool of water, where he fell in love with his reflection (Symington, 1993). Unable to consummate his love, Narcissus "lay gazing enraptured into the pool, hour after hour," fell into the pool and drowned, and finally changed into a flower that bears his name, the narcissus. This term narcissism must not be confused with the term *egocentrism*, which is a preoccupation with one's own internal world (Windschitl, Rose, Stalkfleet & Smith, 2008). The term has been applied in contemporary psychology to personality, and *the narcissistic personality disorder* is the person who loves him/herself above all else, and that's all that matters in the world, and is usually considered a problem in a person or group's relationships with self and others. The only thing the narcissist is interested in is self.

There are several clinical and pathological types of narcissistic personality disorders that are beyond the scope of this discussion, but the *narcissistic rage* applicable to the adolescents on this football team occurs on a continuum from instances of aloofness, and expression of mild irritation or annoyance, to serious outbursts, including violent attacks (Malmquist, 2006). There is often a delusional element in narcissism, in which the individual has a grossly inflated or unrealistic perception of self. This kind of narcissism was a characteristic of the adolescent footballers in the team and manifested as *grand standing*, and *indecision*, the so-called "flip-flop." In colloquial Jamaican patois this is often referred to as "*crowd ass*" behaviour, often resulting in "playing to the gallery" yielding fruitless footballing endeavours. The narcissistic players found it impossible to play as a team, with the name-calling and interpersonal abuse as significant features of their team activity. The psychological defence mechanisms of *projection* and *denial* were characteristic of the team's behaviour, and are characteristics of narcissistic behaviour.

Team building and centring

In the brief time period that I had to work with this team, I had to teach them the characteristic stages of group development – *forming, storming, norming and performing* (Tuckman, 1965). There is a technique that I have developed over the years in cultural therapy, (Hickling, 2012) which I have called *centring*. This daily "warm-up" cultural therapy exercise is held before each major activity session. Borrowed from the warm-up process utilised by actors, dancers and athletes, the purpose of this process is to provide therapy in itself by stimulating physical exercise, removing inhibitions, facilitating self-confidence, and to encourage collective activity. The process also sensitises and prepares participants for the rigorous therapeutic activities to follow. By gathering people in a group in a circle in this way it is a phenomenal way of focusing the team's physical and psychological energies. And so you'll notice many football teams, and cricket teams and athletic teams now starting to use the circle as a dynamic form, before they start to play a game and also at the conclusion of the game. The roles of the team developmental process are to provide a purpose for the team, to build a star team, not a team of stars, to establish shared ownership, develop full respect for each member, make work interesting, develop a self-management team, motivate and inspire team members, lead and facilitate, monitor but not micromanage. The basis of the team management developmental process is a matrix of psychological processes focusing on the need to develop strong social systems and teamwork, and institutional conflict solving.

The sensational defeat of Brazil by Germany in the Semi-Finals of the 2014 World Cup mentioned in chapter 4 is a seminal illustration of the psychology of team cohesion on the football team. Without its captain midfield defensive pillar Thiago Silva due to a double yellow card suspension, and stellar striker Neymar da Silva Santos who was absent having suffered a broken back, the brittle young Brazilian team simply fell apart under the *blitzkrieg* of the clinically brilliant marauding German football team, suffering a humiliating 7-1 defeat in front of their homeland supporters and worldwide fans. Wood (2014) speaks cogently about the humiliating defeat:

Brazil's dramatic meltdown at the semi-finals of the 2014 FIFA World Cup was a classic paradox of maintaining a 'winning' focus, instead of simply performing in the moment. Performance, in any discipline, requires engagement. When we shift attention from the task at hand to something that may, or may not, happen in the future, we undermine our ability to perform 'in the moment'. This is when we typically experience momentary lapses in performance due to poor decision-making, hindered motor control, or lack of concentration. When our attention shifts to outcome, we are also likely to experience heightened hindering anxiety or, potentially, complacency – with both having adverse effects on our ability to perform. Perhaps the loss of two key players and the immense pressure to perform, set anxiety and arousal levels too high before the teams even made it on to the field. For the Brazilian team today, the moment seemed to overwhelm them.

Psychology and gender

Men and women are different in many respects, but in terms of the functioning of the brain, and most areas of psychology, the genders operate identically. There are certain specific psychological issues that apply to women more than to men, but these differences are marginal in the broad scope of things. Women need certain types of psychological interventions that may differ from those that apply to men. Women in Jamaican culture are responsible for bringing up the children and often-times they treat the boys differently from the girls. Sometimes there is a level of psychological abuse that comes from some women that really needs to be dealt with. However, most psychological interventions work equally for men and for women and are needed for both.

The outcome of case study 2

After the single group psychotherapeutic intervention at Connolley House, the football team went on to advance to the semifinals in the Manning Cup that year, as one of the most improved school team in the competition. Following the meeting, I had no further contact with the team but monitored their outcome and progress through the news media. Nearly 30 years later, while shopping at a supermarket, a man approached me and asked if I remembered the group psychotherapeutic session held in my office with that schoolboy football team. He then informed me that the session had made such an insightful effect on the entire team that they almost won the Manning Cup that year; and that all the players who were on the team, had personally transformed their lives, developing into stellar graduates of their school, and subsequently into very successful professionals and members of their respective societies.

Case Study 3: Psychiatric Focus on the Society

Few realise the profound penetration of psychiatry and psychology into every aspect of life. Psychiatry has a far-reaching effect on the society and a concomitant effect on the beautiful game of football. Within recent years, the UWI has carried out significant research on the study of personality disorders in Jamaican society, and makes the linkage between these forms of mental disorders and the facilitation of virulent pathogens that have the potential to destroy the very fabric of our society (see for example, Hickling & Paisley, 2013; Hickling & Walcott, 2013; Hickling, Walcott & Paisley, 2013; Walcott & Hickling, 2013). These works show that people who have personality disorders in the Jamaican culture display problems with power – power struggles, and profound difficulties in managing authority and interpersonal conflict. Persons with these conditions also have unresolved psycho-sexual anxiety, and behavioural problems with physiological and psychological dependency (Hickling & Paisley, 2011). Our studies show that 41 per cent of people in Jamaica are eligible for a diagnosis of personality disorder (Hickling &Walcott, 2013). This finding means that almost one million of the Jamaican population will demonstrate behavioural features and symptoms of a personality disorder at some time in their life.

There are many different categories/types of personality disorders, and persons with these conditions display impulsivity, disregard of the rights and boundaries of others and constantly repeating failure. Applying these definitions of personality disorder to the long-standing struggle for power and authority within the Jamaican culture, and the high levels of verbal and physical aggression in our society, reveals the profound relationship of psychiatry in the Jamaican socio-cultural context. The long-standing struggle for power and authority within the Jamaican culture with high levels of verbal and physical aggression have been associated with serious personality disorders in the culture. The narcissistic personality disorder (inflated sense of self importance and an extreme preoccupation with one's self) is a common feature in many Jamaican sporting teams. Personality disorders in sports produce anger, conflicts, clashes, physical conflict and aggression, and often varying degrees of predatory behaviour.

Translating this to the many sporting activities and differing sports teams in our society we can now begin to understand the repeated failure of many Jamaican sporting teams. There is an increasing need for the presence of the psychiatrist and the psychologist in helping various sporting teams in the supervision of their performance, and calibrating their power management problems! We need to learn how to develop strong social systems of teamwork, accountability and institutional conflict solving. Examination of the performance of many of our teams illustrates the conundrum. The West Indies Cricket Team is a significant case in point. Many of the players exhibit characteristics of personality disorder as we have defined them, and they cannot work effectively with each other. The players often quarrel with each other, and exhibit continuous conflict within the team. The team consists of these brilliant stars, fantastic players, but put together as a team, they are unable to work together. Most teams in the Caribbean have this problem. Everybody is looking at the big problem but is unable to see the whole. This lack of insight is what the Rastafarian calls that lack of *overstanding* which is a neologism for gaining insight. Certainly in the Caribbean we have to struggle against the stigma of engaging psychiatrists and psychologists in our team management. Psychiatrists and psychologists are needed in every area in this society to help to solve the problems that have existed in the Caribbean for centuries! The engagement of teamwork and productivity enhancement, often engender conflict; and conflict arises from the difficulty in managing power and impulse control. Leadership conflict that exists in our football!

Case Study 4: Psychiatric Focus on the International

This case study takes the national endeavour into the international domain. Psychiatry and psychology encompasses the individual to the group; the national to the international with psychiatry and psychology participating in every aspect of life. The international arena in the Caribbean context must address sport and political liberation. One of the Caribbean's most famous political psychologists C.L.R. James has written a profound, phenomenal polemic about the political psychology of cricket in the Caribbean (James, 1993). James was cricket's philosopher king and he identified the problems that devolved from the Caribbean slave environmental work situation, as that phenomenon which has created our present difficulties in working with teams and working with each other. The feature documentary about the great West Indies cricket team of the 1970s and 1980s *Fire in Babylon* (Riley, 2010) describes how the leadership of Clive Lloyd used psychology and combined it with the politics of the time, to weld together a team of cricketers in the 1970s who became famous around the world. The documentary describes the fast bowlers, the batsmen, and the political strategy used by this team to dominate world cricket that culminated in the description of the 'Black Wash' of England in 1984 (Cooke, 2011). The documentary also highlights the political esteem that is embedded in sports, and underlines the political value which Caribbean people need to capture in themselves, to negate the difficult experiences they encounter.

I worked for six months in 1993 as a consultant psychiatrist in Palmerston North situated in New Zealand's North Island and was exposed to the culture of the Maori people who were the original aboriginal people in that country. Many aspects of Maori culture have become a part of the cultural fabric of New Zealand in the post-colonial period. The famous rugby football team of New Zealand, the All Blacks, has accommodated the Maori traditional ceremonial war-dance called the *Haka* into its warm-up routine. Performed at the start of each game by the All Blacks team, the "Ka Mate" version of the Haka is a vigorous dance accompanied by blood curdling yells and chants that communicate to the opposing team "yuh naa go firighten we; yuh naa go fight we down and yuh naa go overpower we, because we stronger dan unno" (You are not going to frighten us, you are not going to fight us down and you are not going to overpower us because we are stronger than all of you).

Integrating the psychiatrist into the football team

There is a major difference between a psychiatrist and a psychologist. This major difference is that the psychiatrist is trained in medicine and therefore has a whole armamentarium of pharmacology and therapeutics that are available to him, that's not available to a psychologist. Both the psychiatrist and the clinical psychologist are trained in the recognition and treatment of mental disorders. The psychologist, in the main, is trained in mental wellness and its enhancement. Both of these professionals have to know a lot about mental disorders, and have to work together in resolving mental challenges. So the psychologist and the psychiatrist must be integrated into the total team and must both be inculcated into the coaching organisation of sporting teams.

There are a number of coaches in this country, for example, that won't have a psychologist on the team because of their own stubborn narcissism. A case study from a local psychologist at this conference illustrates the point (Charles, 2014b, personal communication):

> I was the psychologist incorporated into a local school Manning Cup Team programme and the coach and I had a very good relationship. After he retired, the new coach who succeeded him felt that the coach is the only person who is supposed to speak to the players. The manager of the team told me that the new coach had indicated that he did not need a psychologist on the team, because he was a psychologist. After I became disengaged from the team, there was a situation, at the end of regulation time of a game where the team went into penalty kicks. The boys from the team kicked away all the penalties, they were all so nervous. I was no longer a part of the team, and was not there to help to calm their anxieties at that crucial moment. Now I have been volunteering with a female football team, to train them in improving mental skills. We have been working on technical skills, and communication and organisation. We need to incorporate mental skills into Jamaican sports in general and football in particular, if we are to move forward. All major teams across the world have mental health professionals working with them.

Talent without organisation

The recent FIFA World Cup football competition in Brazil 2014 has illustrated, exquisitely, how football, the beautiful game, can inspire a nation, a continent. The beautiful game can help to 'brand' a country. The famous Jamaican football player and coach Muggy Graham, who attended the conference, has always said that anytime there is a major Manning Cup football match in Jamaica, there is no murder committed in the country, and that there is a reduction in crime across the country (Graham, 2013). There is no doubt that sports, like music and other aspects of our culture, have helped to create and establish a 'Brand Jamaica' which is famous and compelling worldwide, far in excess of the tiny size of our country. The success of the Reggae Boys in the World Cup of 1998 in France (see chapter 8) also illustrates the importance of the application of psychology and psychiatry to inspire the Jamaican people in order to transform them to new level of excellent productivity.

Jamaican reggae musician Robert Nesta Marley has already contributed, in part, to the brand Jamaica and to the catalysis of this transformation process of the Jamaican people. Our people have to *overstand* that it's not just talented people that are required to solve the myriad problems in Jamaica, but all of us learning to work together in teams must be the primacy of the task facing this nation. Usain Bolt, Shelly-Ann Fraser-Pryce and a myriad other Jamaican elite athletes who have made unbelievable impact in world athletics have demonstrated the synthesis of the presence of the talent and the need for careful organisation to work with their coaching teams to achieve success. The talent of the Jamaican people needs to be harnessed. If Usain Bolt didn't have a Glen Mills as a coach would his legendary talents have been harnessed? Glen Mills is one of the greatest coaches we have ever had, in this country, perhaps in the world. The psychologist and the psychiatrist have to help our athletes and teams to learn self-control and to acquire self-confidence.

The Reggae Boys football team is now on that path in their process of rebuilding under the guidance of new coach Winfried Schäfer. Being home grown and locally trained is just one part of the way forward. However the psychological *overstanding* of the world and the organisational *overstanding* of global politics and economics, in particular the White world, must provide the gestalt of our success. In Jamaica we are training and learning not only to work in a Black world, but also to work in a White-dominated world. We have to gather intelligence; to know exactly what's going on in the world; we have to be able to speak several languages. We have to recruit talent from various countries of the world to help us come to maturity in this particular struggle. Bob Marley wasn't only a phenomenal musician, lyricist and singer, he was a footballer in his own right. Jamaican footballer of the 1970s Allan "Skill" Cole, friend, confidant, manager and co-producer of Marley, and who was a speaker at this football conference, has said that Bob Marley was bringing the Corner League to the World Cup (Davis, 2013). In going from the corner league to the World Cup we have to recognise that success is not only about talent, but it's about organisation and it's about team management. Psychology and psychiatry within the sport of football are keys to this *overstanding* which must take place within the context of the professionalisation of football in the Caribbean.

Chapter 10

Caribbean Football: The Way Forward

Christopher A.D. Charles

This chapter brings together information from the previous chapters and the discourse at the conference to chart a way forward for Caribbean football. The issues discussed briefly are developing local coaches and football philosophies, establishing long-term and integrated football programmes, and the professionalisation of football, creation of a cadre of long-term technical staff, establishment of participatory governance structures, promotion of gender equality, and the use of football to improve learning in schools and promote community development.

Develop Local Coaches

We do not have to rely on foreign coaches and managers such as Brazilian Réne Simões in Jamaica in 1998 and German Winfried Schäfer presently, and Dutchman Leo Beenhakker in Trinidad and Tobago in 2006, to qualify for the World Cup. The Caribbean has done exceptionally well internationally in the sports of cricket, netball and track and field without any reliance on foreign coaches. The same can be achieved in football with local coaches and administrators. These administrators and coaches should assess what is being done in cricket, netball and track and field administratively and technically and strive for similar excellence in football. Football federations throughout the region should stipulate that within an agreed period of time all coaches should be FIFA certified and learn teaching methodology with the ultimate goal of becoming trained teachers. Football is about motivating, instructing and guiding the players to grow and develop and give of their best in every game. Coaching is a scientific teaching enterprise which requires training.

Develop a Football Philosophy and a Unique Style of Play

Each Caribbean country needs to develop a football philosophy about what football means to the nation and what the country's approach to the game is. This philosophy should not be fixed in stone but change over time as the game evolves. A guiding football philosophy means that every coach of a particular national team would work within the framework of this philosophy. Related to this absence of a football philosophy is the lack of a unique style of play. All great national football teams that have played consistently well at the World Cup not only have a football philosophy but also a unique style of play that separates these teams from other teams. These styles are also modified and changed over time as is required. Brazil changed its philosophical approach to the game and modified its style of play after the team failed to win the 1982 World Cup in Mexico. We, too, need to develop our own philosophies and styles of play in the Caribbean.

Create Long-term, Integrated Football Programmes

Long-term developmental football programmes are needed in the Caribbean. These football programmes should run from the primary/ preparatory school level to high school to the professional clubs. Residential football schools should be created in the region where the youngsters learn and practise the requirements of the game every morning and then go to classes for the regular academic subjects. What we have in the Caribbean are competitions rather than developmental programmes. For example, in Jamaica youngsters play at the preparatory school level, and then in high school they play the Pepsi and Colts competitions followed by the Manning or DaCosta Cup competitions. These are football competitions at different levels but they are not a part of a structured and comprehensive national football programme where we get the youngsters to a certain standard by a certain age based on international standards. Generally, the schoolboy footballers who graduate from high school in the region do not have the skills to make any of the top football clubs in the world. Stern John, Dwight Yorke and Russell Latapy, Lindy Delapenha, Allan Cole, Ricardo Fuller, Don Davis, Shaka Hislop and Ricardo Gardener, and so on, are the exceptions. These Caribbean footballers played for international clubs not because of a comprehensive football programme at home but because of their exceptional talent, hard work and discipline.

We must focus on developing speed and pace because many Caribbean footballers cannot cope with the speed and pace of international play. The development of pace and speed should not be a problem for Caribbean footballers to acquire because the region has a rich athletic tradition. The techniques to acquire pace and speed for international football should be learnt from the internationally renowned athletic coaches in the region. The expertise exists in the Caribbean to get the players in the physical conditioning required for the speed and pace of high quality international play.

The other important factor is diet. The "box food" or fast food diet which is the staple of many Caribbean footballers is bad for their health. Players have to start eating healthy and eating for the rigorous physical demands of international football. This is where nutritionists are needed to guide the process of healthy eating among footballers so they can perform effectively at the international level.

The discipline of players is another crucial factor. This discipline must be seen in its broadest sense to encompass appropriate social behaviour, appropriate behaviour at training, appropriate professional behaviour, and the intrinsic motivation to personally train and improve one's skill and physical conditioning. Players who lack discipline are not coachable. Therefore, young players should be socialised from early about the discipline required to play football thereby making them coachable. Caribbean players will not survive with international clubs without discipline no matter how talented they are.

Professionalisation: Make Football a Business

Caribbean states need to move football from a way of life to a business of life in the way that FIFA moved from being a global governing body of football to a global business and the game has been professionalised in Trinidad and Tobago. Professionalisation of football in the Caribbean means players would now see football as their livelihood so they would give more to the sport. Young players with the passion, skill and talent for football would be able to look towards a possible career in professional football at home. Professionalisation of the sport would raise the standard of play in the region and raise the prestige of the sport and attract more private sector sponsorship. The professional clubs would have their developmental football programmes that would produce more footballers that could play for the top football clubs in the world. A professional football league would not be financially viable in each Eastern Caribbean State because of their small size . The football federations in the organisation of Eastern Caribbean States (OECS) should in act in concert to establish a professional football league for the Eastern Caribbean.

Build an Integrative Cadre of Long-term Technical Staff

The typical staff accompanying national teams to an overseas football competition, depending on funds available, generally include the coaches/technical directors, the manager, the team doctor and the physiotherapist. The doctors and the physiotherapists usually work only when the team has a game, but they need to be fully integrated into the team. Some teams do not have a nutritionist. All teams should have nutritionists to guide the players about the kind of diet required to play football at the highest level. Sport psychiatrists and sport psychologists are also very important members of the technical staff that many Caribbean national teams do not have. These mental health professional not only deal with behavioural problems and mental disorders that may manifest themselves and create team problems but also teach players mental skills to improve their performance. The team doctor, physiotherapist, nutritionist, sport psychiatrists or psychologist should be integrated as long-term technical staff so that their collective effort with the coaching staff will yield big dividends over time for Caribbean football.

Establish Participatory Governance Structures

The authoritarian style of leadership is very common in the Caribbean where people in positions of power are terse and insensitive towards subordinates and constituents. These leaders do not share information or listen to any one because the organisation they run is their fiefdom. Therefore, they administer programmes without any accountability. Many of the football federations in the region are run by authoritarians. This style of leadership is counter-productive for football. Only those in the leadership structure are allowed to make a contribution while other people in the society with the skills and experience to contribute to football are prevented or discouraged from doing so. Participatory governance structures in the football associations and federations in the various Caribbean territories are needed because this style of leadership facilitates broad-based contributions and well-informed leadership that utilises all the talent that is available in the service of football rather than the non-participatory one don style of governance.

Use Football to Promote Gender Equality

Football should be used as a vehicle for cultural change in the region in the service of gender equality. Adequate administrative, technical and financial support should be given to women footballers and the sport used as a symbol of gender equality in the region. Football is the most popular sport in the Caribbean so changes towards gender equality in this sport will further the cause of gender equality. A female football competition should be encouraged at the primary and secondary school levels throughout the region. Children seeing girls playing football from an early age will accept women playing football as a natural phenomenon. Moreover, the earlier the football developmental trajectory for women, the more likely it is that Caribbean countries will qualify for the Women's World Cup.

Use Football to Improve Learning in Schools

In many schools across the Caribbean there is a dichotomy between academics and sports where teachers and parents socialise children to see academics as superior and sports as inferior. In addition, students who are not doing well academically are encouraged to do sports. Sports in general, and football in particular, require a scientific approach to excel. Football should be seen as an academic pursuit given the scientific/technical understanding of the game and the skills required in order to play the game well. Football (like all sports) should be used to teach life lessons like team work, role requirements, the interrelationship of various roles, performing in the spotlight, performing under pressure, working well with others including those with whom you have disagreements and conflicts. The values of fair play, and respecting authority can also be taught, and the importance of leadership by example because high school footballers are the most popular students in schools. Learning how to deal with setbacks and defeats as well as successes are important life skills. The importance of commitment, hard work and doing one's best are also important lessons that youngsters learn from football. Football should be used to enhance academic instructions in schools and more importantly as a tool towards the total development and well-being of students.

Use Football to Mobilise for Community Development
Football used in the appropriate way can be a vehicle that unites warring factions in a community. A football team can be created with players from all sides in the conflict so the former enemies can work towards a common goal as a team to defeat other teams. There is less crime and violence in communities when the youngsters are engaged in football. There is also less crime when national teams are playing or the youth are watching World Cup Football. The passion of the youth for football should be harnessed in ways that promote unity, cooperation, peace, and community mobilisation in support of development. Throughout the Caribbean baby showers and christenings, engagements and weddings, deaths and important milestones in life are celebrated partly with a dance or fete. Football games should be added to these celebratory events so youngsters have more opportunities to play the game and see it as an important life ritual in the community.

References

Ainsworth, M. & Bowlby, J. (1965).
Child care and the growth of love. London: Penguin Books.

Anderson, B. (1991).
Imagined communities. Verso: London.

Antunes, A. (2013).
The cost of corruption in Brazil could be up to $53 billion just this year. *Forbes,* 28 November. Retrieved from http://www.forbes.com/sites/andersonantunes/2013/11/28/the-cost-of-corruption-in-brazil-could-be-up-to-53-billion-just-this-year-alone/.

Armstrong, G. (1999).
Football cultures and identities. Basingstoke: Macmillan.

Atluri, T. L. (2001).
When the closet is a nation: Homophobia, heterosexism and sexism in the Commonwealth Caribbean. Cave Hill: Centre of Gender and Development, UWI.

Back, L., Crabbe, T. & Solomos, J. (1998).
Lions, black skins and reggae gyals: Race, nation and identity in football. London: Goldsmith College, University of London.

Bailey, E. & Muller, N. (1998).
Jamaica's reggae boys: World Cup 1998. Kingston: Ian Randle Publishers and Creative Communications Inc.

Bailey, R. (2008).
Barnes looking to instill Jamaican philosophy. *Jamaica Gleaner,* 4 November. Retrieved from http://jamaica-gleaner.com/gleaner/20081104/sports/sports1.html.

Bandura, A. (1997).
Self-Efficacy: The exercise of control. New York: Freeman.

Barbara, V. (2014).
Pity Brazil's military police. The *New York Times,* 19 February. Retrieved from http://www.nytimes.com/2014/02/20/opinion/barbara-reform-brazils-military-police.html?_r=0.

Barrow, C. (1998).
Caribbean portraits. Kingston: Ian Randle Publishers.

Beckford, G. (2000).
Persistent Poverty. Kingston: University of the West Indies.
Beckford, O. (2009).
The sociology of crime. Paper presented at Caribbean Studies Association Conference in Barbados.
Beckles, H. M. & Stoddart, B. (1995).
Liberation cricket West Indies cricket culture: A purely natural extension: Women's cricket culture. Kingston: Ian Randle Publishers.
Bell, R. (2009).
Keynote address at Jackie Bell K.O. award presentation. 26 March. Retrieved from http://www.ksafa.net/Archives/News_Mar26JB_09.htm.
Berger, P. L. & Huntington, S.P. (2002).
Many globalizations: Cultural diversity in the contemporary world. New York: Oxford University Press.
Bertalanffy, L.V (1972).
The history and status of general systems theory. *Academy of Management Journal, 15,* 407-426,
Bonater, D. (2013).
Gangs, gunfights loom over Rio de Janeiro World Cup Preparation 29th December. *Telegraph,* 29 December. Retrieved from http://www.telegraph.co.uk/news/worldnews/southamerica/brazil/10541252/Gang-gunfights-loom-over-Rio-de-Janeiros-World-Cup-preparations.html.
Bourne, C.O.E. (2005).
Poverty and its alleviation in the Caribbean. Retrieved from http://www.caribank.org/uploads/publications-reports/statements-and-speeches/dr-compton-bourne/BournePoverty.pdf.
Boyd, A. (2014).
Schäffer: Caribbean Cup very important. *Jamaica Gleaner,* 26 October 2014. Retrieved from http://jamaica-gleaner.com/gleaner/20141026/sports/sports1.html.
Braveboy-Wagner, J.A. (1993).
The Caribbean in the Pacific century. Boulder: Lynne Rienner Publishers.
British Broadcasting Corporation. (2014).
Roy Hodgson recruits psychiatrist Dr Steve Peters for England. 4 March.

Retrieved from http://www.bbc.com/sport/0/football/26435483.

Brobst, B. & Ward, P. (2002).
Effects of public posting, goal setting, and oral feedback on the skills of female soccer players. *Journal of Applied Behaviour Analysis*, 35, 247-257.

Burdsey, D. & Chappell, R. (2003).
Soldiers, sashes and shamrocks: Football and social identity in Scotland and Northern Ireland. *Sociology of Sports Online*, 6,1.

Burdsey, D. (2009).
Forgotten fields? Centralizing the experiences of minority ethnic men's football clubs in England. *Soccer & Society,10*, 704-721.

Butcher, R. (2014).
Personal communication.

Butler, J. (1999).
Gender trouble: Feminism and the subversion of identity. New York: Routledge.

Butler, J. (2009).
Performativity precariety and sexual policies. *AIBR. Revista de AntropologÃa Iberoamericana,4*, 1-13.

Campbell, P.I. (2014).
A ('black') historian using sociology to write a history of 'black' sport: a critical reflection. *Qualitative Research in Sport, Exercise and Health*, DOI: 10.1080/2159676X.2014.949834.

Chai, S. (2011).
Theories of culture, cognition, and action. In I.C. Jarvie & J. P. Zamora-Bonilla (eds.), *The Sage handbook of the philosophy of social sciences* (pp.487-496).Thousand Oaks, CA: Sage Publications.

Charles, A. (2002).
Social sciences course material: Theories in economic development EC22A. Bridgetown: Distance Education Centre.

Charles, C. (2002).
Garrison communities as counter societies: The case of the 1998 Zeeks' Riot in Jamaica. *Ideaz, 1*, 30-43.

Charles, C.A.D. (2004).
Political identity and criminal violence in Jamaica: The garrison community of August Town and the 2002 Election. *Social and Economic Studies, 53*, 31-74.

Charles, C.A.D. & Beckford, O. (2012).
The informal justice system in garrison constituencies. *Social and Economic Studies*, *61*,51-72.
Charles, C.A.D. (2014a).
Football and the construction and maintenance of self among female footballers. Unpublished paper.
Charles, C.A.D. (2014b).
Personal communication.
C.I.A. (2008).
World factbook. Grenada demographic profile. Retrieved from www.indexmundi.com.
C.I.A. (2013).
World factbook. Retrieved from https://www.cia.gov/library/publications/download/download-2013/index.html.
Clanchie, P. (1998).
Football, instability and passion. *Communications*, 67, 9-23.
Cohen, A. (1989).
The symbolic construction of community. London: Routledge.
Cooke, M. (2011).
Fire in Babylon' documentary captures West Indies cricket peak. *Jamaica Gleaner*, 11 April. Retrieved from http://jamaica-gleaner.com/gleaner/20110411/ent/ent2.html.
Cole, A. (2014).
Personal communication.
Condato, A. N.(2006).
A political history of Brazilian transition from military dictatorship to democracy. *Rev. Sociol*, 2,1-33.
Cowan, S. (2014).
Sponsors blown away by LIME street football challenge. *Jamaica Observer*, 27 May. Retrieved from http://www.jamaicaobserver.com/sport/Sponsors-blown-away-by-LIME-Street-Football-Challenge_16745622.
Creswell, J.W. & Miller, D.L. (2000).
Determining validity in qualitative inquiry. *Theory into Practice*, *39*, 124-130.
Creswell, J.W. (2008)
Educational Research. 3rd Edition, New Jersey: Pearson/ Merrill Prentice.

Croxton, J.S. & Klonsky, B.G. (1982).
Sex differences in causal attributions for success and failure in real and hypothetical sport settings. *Sex Roles, 8,* 399-409.

Davies, J. (2013).
The rising importance of football philosophy in the Premiere League. English Premier League Index, 20 March. Retrieved from http://eplindex.com/28893/rising-importance-footballing-philosophy-epl.html.

Davies, J. (2012).
System football: Part two. 10 November. Retrieved from http://tikitakafootballcoaching.wordpress.com/2012/11/10/systems-football-part-two.

Davies, J. (2014).
20 changes in football since World Cup '98. 3 March. Betting expert blog. Retrieved from http://www.bettingexpert.com/blog/20-changes-in-football.

Davis, D. (2012).
Football coaches playing music chairs in Jamaica. Don D Soccer Coaching School. 10 December. Retrieved from https://www.facebook.com/permalink.php?story_fbid=431441626911115&id=241117712610175.

Davis, D. (2013).
From Emancipation to the reggae boys. Kingston: Conscious Movement Publications.

Davis, D. (2014).
Personal communication.

Dawes, K. (2004).
Natural mysticism. Leeds: Peepal Tree Press.

Dilley, P. (2000).
Conducting successful interviews: Tips for intrepid research. *Theory into Practice, 39,*124-130.

Dixon, K. (2011).
A third way for football fandom research: Anthony Giddens and structuration Theory. *Journal of Soccer & Society, 12,* 279-298.

Downs, A. (2004).
Boys of the empire: Elite education and the socio-cultural

construction of hegemonic masculinity in Barbados, 1875-1920. In R. Reddock (ed.), *Interrogating Masculinities* (pp. 105-136). Kingston, Jamaica: University of the West Indies Press.

Duke, V., & Crolley, L. (1996).
Football, nationality and the state. London: Addison Wesley Longman.

Dunning, E., Murphy, P., & Williams, J. (1988).
The roots of football hooliganism. London: Routledge and Kegan Paul.

Earle, R. & Davies, D. (1998).
One love: The story of Jamaica's reggae boys and the 1998 World Cup. London: Andre Deutsch Ltd.

Eisenberg, C. (2006).
FIFA 1975-2000: the business of a football development organisation. *History Social Research, 31*, 55-68.

Fallon, M. & Butterfield, K. (2012).
The influence of unethical peer behaviour on observers' unethical behaviour: A social cognitive perspective. *Journal of Business Ethics, 109*, 117-131.

Ferguson, J. (2006).
World class. An illustrated history of Caribbean football. Oxford: McMillan.

Ferrara de Souza, P.H.G.(2010).
Poverty, inequality and social policies in Brazil 1995-2009. Institute of Applied Economic Research. Retrieved from http://www.ipc-undp.org/pressroom/files/ipc631.pdf.

Ferreira, F.H.G., Velez, C.E. & de Barros, R.P. (2004).
Inequality and economic development in Brazil. Washington, DC: World Bank.

Fryer, P. (1984).
Staying power: The history of black people in Britain. London: Pluto Press.

FIFA.(2014a).
History of football-the origins. Retrieved from http://www.fifa.com/classicfootball/history/the-game/origins.html.

FIFA. (2014b).
FIFA futsal World Cup final. Retrieved from http://www.fifa.com/tournaments/archive/futsalworldcup/index.html.

FIFA. (2014c).

Competitions. Retrieved from http://www.fifa.com/tournaments/
archive/futsalworldcup/index.html.

Football Associations. (2014).

The history of the FA. Retrieved from http://www.thefa.com/about-
football-association/history.

Franklyn, D. (2009).

Sprinting into history: Jamaica and the 2008 Olympic Games.
Kingston: Wilson, Franklyn, Barnes.

Freedman, A. (2014).

Suarez defends his World Cup biting incident: Says he fell into Italian defender.
Retrieved from http://mashable.com/2014/06/28/suarez-defends-his-
world-cup-biting-incident-says-he-fell-into-italian-defender/.

Gayle, H. (2014).

Personal communication.

Geddes, T. (1998a).

Jamaican soccer star apologizes, asks understanding. *Sun–Sentinel.*
24 May. Retrieved from http://articles.sun-sentinel.com/1998-05-
24/sports/9805230266_1_jamaican-world-cup-antigua retrieved
11 February 2014.

Geddes,T.(1998b).

Reggae Boys play at Giant stadium. *Sun Sentinel*, 31 May.
Retrieved from http://articles.sun-sentinel.com/1998-05-31/
sports/9805300210_1_world-cup-trinidad-coca-cola-fifa.

Geddes, T. (1999).

Jamaica glows from Reggae Boyz play in the World Cup.
Sun Sentinel, 17 January. Retrieved from http://articles.sun-
sentinel.com/1999-01-17/sports/9901160294_1_world-cup-
finals-test-series-jamaica.

Geo, R.W. & Noonan,S. (2007).

The sociology of community. In Bryant, C. D. & Peck, D. L.
(eds.). *21st Century Sociology* (pp. 455-465). Thousand Oaks:
SAGE Publications, Inc.

Gerronel, R. (2013).

Forbes starting lineup: The 11 richest soccer billionaires. *Forbes
Magazine*, 12 March. Retrieved from http://www.forbes.com/

sites/ricardogeromel/2013/03/12/forbes-starting-lineup-the-11-richest-soccer-billionaires/.

Gertler, P., Heckman, J., Pinto,R., Zanolini, A., Vermeersch,C., Walker, S., Chang, S.& Grantham-McGregor, S.(2013).
Labor market returns to early childhood stimulation: A 20-year follow-up to an experimental intervention in Jamaica. Working Paper 19185. Retrieved from http://www.nber.org/papers/w19185.

Gillespie,S., Haddad, L., Mannar,V.; Menon,P. & Nisbett, N. (2012).
The politics of reducing malnutrition: building commitment and accelerating progress. *The Lancet.* Retrieved from http://dx.doi.org/10.1016/S0140-6736(13)60842-9.

Girvan, N. (2001).
Reinterpreting the Caribbean. In B. Meeks and Folk Lindahl (eds.), *New Caribbean Thought.* (pp.3-23). Jamaica: University of the West Indies Press.

Giddens, A. & Held, D. (1982).
Classes, power, and conflict: Classical and contemporary debates. Berkeley and Los Angeles: University of California Press.

Giulianotti, R. & Robertson, R. (2009).
Globalisation and football. London: Sage Publications Ltd.

Giroux, H. (2000).
Public pedagogy cultural politics: Stuart Hall and the crisis of culture. *Cultural Studies, 14,* 341-345.

Glaser. T. (2007).
Road to France 1998: Remembering the glory. *Jamaica Gleaner,* 17 November. Retrieved from http://jamaica-gleaner.com/gleaner/20071117/sports/sports2.html.

Golesworthy, M. (1972).
We are the champions: A history of the football league champions 1888-1972. London: Pelham Books.

Golesworthy, M. (1973).
The encyclopaedia of association football. London: Robert Hale Publishers.

Goncalves, J.T. (1998).
The principles of Brazilian soccer. Spring City: Reedswain Books and Video.

Graham, L. (2013).

Sports – the opium of our high schools. *Jamaica Observer*, 4 May. Retrieved from http://m.jamaicaobserver.com/mobile/business/Sports---the-opium-of-our-high schools_14192172.

Grenada Information Service. (2009).

Minister of Finance contextualizes "disturbing" poverty report. Retrieved from www.gov.gd.

Guinto, M. (2009).

Hope is round and leather: Football unifies a strife-torn Haiti. *Undergraduate Review: a Journal of Undergraduate Student Research, 10,* 4-9.

Hall, S. (1990).

Cultural identity and diaspora. In J. Rutherford (ed.) *Identity: Community, culture, difference.* (pp. 222-37). London: Lawrence and Wishart.

Hall, S. (2001).

Negotiating Caribbean identities. In B. Meeks and F. Lindahl, (eds.) *New Caribbean Thought: A Reader* (pp.24-39). Jamaica: University of the West Indies Press.

Hall, S. (2007).

Resistance through rituals: Youth subcultures in post war Britain. London: Taylor and Francis.

Hamilton, A. & Hinds, R. (1999).

Black pearls: The A-Z of black footballers in the English game. London: Hansib Publications.

Hamilton, D. (2005).

Scotland, the Caribbean and the Atlantic world, 1750-1820. Manchester: Manchester University Press.

Harvey, A. (2005).

Football: The first hundred years: The untold story. New York: Routledge.

Hastie, P. & Saunders, J.E. (1991).

Effects of class size and equipment availability on student involvement in physical education. *The Journal of Experimental Education, 59,* 212-224.

Hickling, F.W.(2012).

Psychohistoriography. A postcolonial psychoanalytic and psychotherapeutic model. London: Jessica Kingsley Publishers.

Hickling F.W. & Paisley V. (2011).

Redefining personality disorder: A Jamaican perspective. *Rev Panam Salud Publica, 1,* 255–61.

Hickling, F.W. &Walcott, G. (2013).

A view of personality disorder from the colonial periphery. *West Indian Medical Journal, 62,* DOI: 10.7727/wimj.2013.122.

Hickling, F.W., Walcott, G. &Paisley, V. (2013).

Shakatani: The phenomenology of personality disorder in Jamaican patients. *West Indian Medical Journal, 62,* DOI: 10.7727/wimj.2012.333.

Hodges, P. (2014).

Increase in couple families. Jamaica Information Service. 16 June. Retrieved from http://jis.gov.jm/increase-couple-families/.

Howe, D. (1998).

It should be cause for celebration that English players with Caribbean parents wish to play for the Jamaican World Cup team. *New Statesman, 127,* 29.

Hughes, L. (1990).

Selected poems of Langston Hughes. New York: Random House.

International Monetary Fund. (2007).

World economic outlook database. Retrieved from: https://www.imf.org/external/pubs/ft/weo/2007/02/weodata/index.aspx.

Ito, T. (1999).

Brazil: History of political economic turmoil. *Washington Post,* January. Retrieved from http://www.washingtonpost.com/wp-srv/inatl/longterm/brazil/overview.htm.

Jarvie, G. & Maguire, J. (1994).

Sport and leisure in social thought. London: Routledge.

Kuethe, T.H. & Motamed, M. (2009).

Returns to stardom: Evidence from U.S. Major League Soccer. Journal of Sports Economics, 11, 567-579.

Knight, F.W. & Palmer, C.A. (1989).

The modern Caribbean. Chapel Hill: University of North Carolina Press.

Hope, D. P. (2010).

Masculinities in the Jamaican dancehall. Kingston: Ian Randle Publishers.

James, C.L.R. (1993).

Beyond a boundary. Durham: Duke University Press.

Kairi Consulting Firm (1998).

Country poverty assessment. St. Georges: Ministry of Finance, Government of Grenada.

KASAFA. (2014).

History of KSAFA women's football competitions. Retrieved from http://ksafa.net/Archives/competitions_W_hstry.htm.

Krauss, W. (2003).

Football, nation and identity: German miracles in the post –war era. In N. Dyck & E. P. Archetti (eds).*Sport, dance and embodied identities* (pp.197-216). Oxford, New York: Berg.

Longman, J. (1997).

Soccer: British quartet rocks Jamaica. *New York Times*, 2 October. Retrieved from http://www.nytimes.com/1997/10/02/sports/soccer-british-quartet-rocks-jamaica.html.

Lowndes, W. (1952).

The story of football. London: Thorsons Publishers.

Laker, A. (2002).

The sociology of sports and physical education: An introduction. London: Taylor &Francis.

Lee, J. (2008).

The lady footballers struggling to play in Victorian Britain. Abington, Oxon: Routledge.

Marcus, J.T. (2009).

Sports law in the Caribbean: Growth and development. *The International Sports Law Journal, 1-2,*140.

Macionis, J. & Plummer, K. (2008).

Sociology: A global introduction. Essex: Pearson Education.

Malmquist,C.P. (2006).

Homicide: A psychiatric perspective. Arlington, VA: American Psychiatric Publishing, Inc.

Mason, N. (1975).

Football: *The story of all the world's football games.* London: Drake Publishers.

Mason, T. (1980).

Association football and English society 1863-1915. Sussex: The Harvester Press Ltd.

Matteucci, I. (2012).

Sport as a cultural model: Italian women's soccer over the past 10 years. *The International Journal of the History of Sports,* 29, 353-373.

Metheny, E. (1965).

Connotations of movement in sport and dance: A collection of speeches about sport and dance as significant forms of human behaviour. Los Angeles: W.C Brown Company.

Mieses, J.A. (1993).

Elections, political parties and political culture in Brazil: Change and continuities. *Journal of Latin American Studies,* 25, 575-611.

Ministry of Finance. (2009).

Consultation on 2010 budget. St. Georges: Government of Grenada.

Mitchell, A. (2013).

The fate of Scotland's first black footballer revealed, 20 March. Retrieved from www.scotsman.com/sport/football/latest/fa

Mohammed, P. (2004).

Unmasking masculinity and deconstructing patriarchy: Problems and possibilities within feminist epistemology. In R. Reddock (ed.), *Interrogating Masculinities* (pp. 38-67). Jamaica: University of the West Indies Press.

Moorhouse, H. (1984).

Professional football and working class culture: English theories and Scottish evidence. *Sociological Review,* 32, 285-315.

Mullock, S. (2014).

Luis Suarez wanted out of Liverpool before his latest bite controversy at the World Cup. *Mirror,* 28 June. Retrieved from http://www.mirror.co.uk/sport/football/transfer-news/luis-suarez-wanted-out-liverpool-3782735.

Murray, B. (1984).

The old firm: sectarianism, sport and society in Scotland. Edinburgh: John Donald Publishers Ltd.

Nettleford, R (1993).

Inward stretch outward reach: A voice from the Caribbean. London and Basingstoke: Macmillan Press.

New Strait Times. (1998a).

Brazilian Simões Jamaica's miracle man. 31 May. Retrieved from http://news.google.com/s?nid=1309&dat=19980531&id=qvVOA AAAIBAJ&sjid=ABUEAAAAIBAJ&pg=3730,3949977.

New Strait Times. (1998b).

Rank outsiders ready to cause a stir. 31 May. Retrieved from http://news.google.com/s?nid=1309&dat=19980531&id=qvVOAAAAI BAJ&sjid=ABUEAAAAIBAJ&pg=6457,3948453.

Norton, S.(2014).

Germany's 12th man at the World Cup: Big data. *The Wall Street Journal*, 10 July. Retrieved from http://blogs.wsj.com/ cio/2014/07/10/germanys-12th-man-at-the-world-cup-big-data/.

Nurse, K. (2004).

Masculinities in transition: Gender and the global problematique. In R. Reddock (ed.), *Interrogating Masculinities* (pp. 3-37). Jamaica: University of the West Indies Press.

Nye, J.S. (2011).

The future of power. New York: Public Affairs.

Parkin, F. (1982).

Social closure and class formation. In A. Giddens, & D. Held (eds.), *Classes, power, and conflict: Classical and contemporary debates.* Berkeley and Los Angeles: University of California Press.

Perro, V.& Szrerman, D. (2005).

The new generation of social programs. February, 2005 (Working Paper) Retrieved from http://ww2.ie.ufrj.br/eventos/pdfs/ seminarios/pesquisa/the_new_generation_of_social_programs_ in_brazil.pdf.

Phillips, F. (1985).

West Indian constitutions: Post-independence reforms. New York: Oceania Publications Inc.

Reuters. (2014b).

Update 1-Federal troops to help Rio battle gang violence in slums. 21 March. Retrieved from http://uk.reuters.com/article/2014/03/21/brazil-violence-rio-idUKL2N0MI1P320140321.

Robinson, R. (1920).

History of the Queen's Park Football Club 1867-1917, Glasgow. Retrieved from http://scottish-football-historical-archive.com/history.

Riley, S.(2010).

Fire in Babylon Retrieved from http://www.imdb.com/title/tt1727790/.

Romero, S.(2014a).

Brazil's latest clash with its urban youth takes place in the mall. *New York Times*, 19 January. Retrieved from http://www.nytimes.com/2014/01/20/world/americas/brazils-latest-clash-with-its-urban-youth-takes-place-at-the-mall.html.

Romero, S. (2014b).

Slum dwellers are defying Brazil's grand design for Olympics. *New York Times*, 4 March. Retrieved from http://www.nytimes.com/2012/03/05/world/americas/brazil-faces-obstacles-in-preparations-for-rio-olympics.html?pagewanted=all.

Romero, S. & Barnes, T. (2014).

Rio grapples with violence against police officers as World Cup nears. *New York Times*, 30 May. Retrieved from http://www.nytimes.com/2014/05/31/world/americas/crime-surges-in-rio-ahead-of-world-cup.html.

Sage, G. (2002).

Global sport and global mass media. In A. Laker (ed.), *The sociology of sport and physical education*(pp.211-233).London: Routledge.

Said, E.(1978).

Orientalism. New York: Pantheon Books.

Sen, A. (1985).

Commodities and capabilities. Amsterdam: Elsevier Press.

Sen, A. (1999).

Development as freedom. New York: Knopf.

Simon, D. (1995).

Social problems and the sociological imagination: A paradigm for analysis. California: Mc Graw-Hill.

Skinner, J., Zakus, D. H., & Cowell, J. (2008).

Development through sport: Building social capital in disadvantaged communities. *Sport Management Review, 11,* 253–275.

Sky Sports. (2014).

World Cup: England must learn from Germany philosophy, says Avram Grant. 15 July. Retrieved from http://www1.skysports.com/football/news/12098/9383114/england-must-learn-from-germany-philosophy-if-they-want-to-develop.

Smith, M.K.(2005).

Bruce W. Tuckman - forming, storming, norming and performing in groups. Retrieved from http://infed.org/mobi/bruce-w-tuckman-forming-storming-norming-*and-performing-in-groups/*.

Smith, S.L.& Ward, P. (2006).

Behavioral interventions to improve performance in collegiate football. *Journal of Applied Behaviour Analysis,* 39,385-391.

Stamp, M. (2014).

LIME street challenge heats up this Sunday. *Jamaica Gleaner,* 15 May. Retrieved from http://jamaicagleaner.mobi/gleaner/20140515/sports/sports8.php.

Stolorow, R.D. (2013).

On the Inconsolability of grief: Time does not heal the wounds of traumatic loss. *Psychology today.* 21 September. Retrieved from http://www.psychologytoday.com/blog/feeling-relating-existing/201309/the-inconsolability-grief.

Swart, K., Bob U., Knott, B.&Salie, M.(2011).

A sport and socio-cultural legacy beyond 2010: A case study of the football foundation of South Africa. *Development Southern Africa, 28,* 415-428.

Swift, D.F. (1970).

The sociology of education. London: Routledge & Keegan Paul.

Symington, N. (1993).

Narcissism: A new theory. London: Karnac Books.

Tamas, A. (2000).

Systems theory in community development. Retrieved from http://www.
tamas.com/samples/source-docs/System_Theory_in_CD.pdf.

Teelucksingh, J.(2005).

The U.S. media and gender relations in the Caribbean. *Peace
Review: A Journal of Social Justice, 17,*207–214.

Thompson, P. (1989).

The nature of work. London: Macmillan.

Time for Action. (1993).

Report of the West Indian Commission. Jamaica: University of
the West Indies Press.

Tomlinson, A. (2007).

Lord, don't stop the carnival: Trinidad and Tobago at the
2006 FIFA World Cup. *Journal of Sports & Social Issues, 31,*
259-282.

Tucker, E. (2006).

That Jamaican philosophy. *The Star,* 27 December. Retrieved
from http://jamaicastar.com/thestar/20061227/sports/
sports3.html.

Tuckman, B. W.(1965).

Developmental sequence in small groups. *Psychological
Bulletin, 63,* 384-89.

United States Census Bureau. (2012).

*Living arrangements of children under 18 Years old: 1960
to present.* 1 July. Retrieved from http://www.census.gov/
population/socdemo/hh-fam/ch5.xls.

Vail, S. E. (2007).

Community development and sport participation. *Journal of
Sport Management, 21,* 571-596.

Vasili, P.(1998).

The first black footballer: Arthur Wharton 1865-1930. London:
Frank Cass Publishers.

Vamplew, W. (1994).

Wogball: Ethnicity and violence in Australian soccer. In R.
Giulianotti & J. Williams (eds.), *Game without frontiers: Football,
identity and modernity* (pp. 207-23). Aldershot: Arena.

Vold, G., Bernard, T. & Snipes, J. (1998).
Theoretical criminology. New York: Oxford University Press.

Wagner, E.A. (1982).
Sport participation in Latin America. *International Review for the Sociology of Sport, 17,* 29-38.

Walcott, G. & Hickling, F.(2013).
Correlates of conflict, power and authority management, aggression and impulse control in the Jamaican population. *West Indian Medical Journal, 62,* DOI: 10.7727/ wimj.2013.123.

Wallerstein, I. (1995).
The modern world system and evolution. *Journal of World Systems Research, 1,* 1-20.

Walker, S. P., Wachs, T.D., Gardner, J.M.,. Lozo, B., Wasserman, G.A., Pollitt, E. & J. A. Carter, J.A.(2007).
Child development: Risk factors for adverse outcomes in developing countries. The Lancet, 369, 145-157.

Walker, S. P., Chang, S.M., Vera-Hernandez, M.,& S. Grantham-McGregor, S. (2011).
Early childhood stimulation benefits adult competence and reduces violent behavior. *Pediatrics, 127,* 849-857.

Walter, T.O., Brown B. & Grabb E.G. (1991).
Ethnic identity and sports participation: A comparative analysis of West Indian and Italian soccer clubs in metropolitan Toronto. *Canadian Ethnic Studies, 23,* 85-96.

Walvin, J. (1994a).
Black people in Britain. In A. H. Tibbles (ed), *Transatlantic slavery: Against human dignity*(pp.79-82). London: HMSO.

Walvin, J. (1994b).
The people's game: The history of football revisited. Edinburgh and London: Mainstream Publishing Company.

Warrick, W.(2014).
Brazil's mindset meltdown a perfect paradox. Retrieved from http:// www.scoop.co.nz/stories/ED1407/S00062/brazils-mindset-meltdown-a-perfect-paradox.htm.

Williams-Raynor, P. (2011).

Missing daddies, criminal kids: Study suggests fathers' absence puts inner-city youths at risk of turning into criminals. *Jamaica Observer*, 15 May. Retrieved from http://www.jamaicaobserver. com/news/missing-daddies--criminal-kids_8800762.

Windschitl P. D., Rose J. P., Stalkfleet, M. T., Smith A. R. (2008).

Are people excessive or judicious in their egocentrism? A modeling approach to understanding bias and accuracy in people's optimism. *Journal of Personality and Social Psychology, 95,* 253–273.

World Bank. (2002).

Jamaica survey of living conditions. Washington, DC: Development Research Group Poverty and Human Resources.

World Bank. (2010).

World development report. Retrieved from http://web.worldbank. org/WBSITE/EXTERNAL/EXTDEC/EXTRESEARCH/S/0 ,contentMDK:23062354~pagePK:478093~piPK:477627~theSit ePK:477624,00.html.

World Bank. (2013).

World development Indicators: Distribution of income or consumption. Retrieved from http://databank.worldbank.org/ data/download/WDI-2013-ebook.pdf.

Wright-Mills, C.(1953).

The sociological imagination. Oxford: Oxford University Press.

Notes on Contributors

Orville W. Beckford is a lecturer in sociology in the Department of Sociology, Psychology and Social Work at the University of the West Indies (UWI), Mona. He teaches Introduction to Sociology, Caribbean Culture, and Industrial Sociology. Orville Beckford worked on the Mona Commons Township Project Social Report for the UWI and received The Excellence in Teaching Award from The Faculty of Social Sciences in 2012-2013. His research interests are institutional building, industrial sociology, and the culture of the inner city.

Olivene Burke is the executive director of Mona Social Services and lecturer in transformational leadership, human resources and learning strategies at the Mona School of Business and Management at the UWI. She has had a distinguished career as an educator, planner, administrator and community development professional. Her research interests include education, human resource management, quality assurance and transformational leadership and management.

Christopher A.D. Charles is a senior lecturer in political psychology in the Department of Government at the UWI, Mona and operates a psychology consultancy in Kingston and is a fellow of the Institute of Cultural Policy and Innovation. He did doctoral training in psychology and political science and holds a Ph.D. in psychology from the City University of New York. His main research interests are sport psychology, criminological psychology, political psychology, and Black identity, body modification, popular culture, and sexuality. Before going to the UWI, he taught at John Jay College of Criminal Justice of the City University of New York, and The King Graduate School at Monroe College in New York.

Wanda M. Costen is a tenured associate professor and the executive director of the School of Hotel and Restaurant Management, in the W.A. Franke College of Business at Northern Arizona University. She teaches human resources, strategic management, US employment law, organizational behaviour, working with diversity, and hospitality and tourism. Her research interests include racial and gender inequality in organizations, women and leadership, managing diversity, strategic human resources, and educational technology.

Frederick W. Hickling is emeritus professor of psychiatry and was educated in medicine at UWI, Mona. He received specialist training in anatomy at St Thomas' Hospital Medical School, University of London, and postgraduate training in psychiatry at UWI and the University of Edinburgh. He helped to establish a unique community psychiatric service and to pioneer cultural therapy in Jamaica in the 1970s. In the 1980s he established a private psychiatric research and clinical service in Kingston, and in the 1990s he helped to shape policy for African Caribbean Mental Health at North Birmingham Mental Health Services, UK. He was head, Section of Psychiatry, UWI, Mona, from 2000 to 2006, and is executive director of the UWI Caribbean Institute of Mental Health and Substance Abuse (CARIMENSA). He was elected a Distinguished Fellow of the American Psychiatric Association in 2008, Fellow of the Royal College of Psychiatrists UK in 2011 and he received the Order of Distinction (Commander) from the Government of Jamaica in 2012.

Dennis Howard is one of Jamaica's most noted ethnomusicologists, possessing over thirty years of experience in the creative industries. A Grammy nominated music producer, Howard holds a Ph.D. in cultural studies and ethnomusicology from the University of the West Indies. He is the managing director of the Institute of Cultural Policy and Innovation and has presented his research in the United States, Brazil, the United Kingdom, Mexico, South Africa and several Caribbean countries.

Karen D. Madden is second vice president of the Press Association of Jamaica and a senior producer with the RJR Communications Group. Her career has spanned administration, journalism and production, focusing on programmes, news and sports. She also has international media experience as stringer for BBC Caribbean. Karen holds a Master of Arts in Cultural Studies and a Bachelor of Arts in Language and

Communication, from the UWI. She has a passionate interest in sports and her research has so far focused on sports in Caribbean culture through the lens of gender. Karen D. Madden is also a past student of the St Andrew High School.

Hilary Robertson-Hickling is a lecturer in Human Resource Management in the Mona School of Business and Management at the UWI, Mona. She was educated at UWI, Johns Hopkins University and the University of Birmingham. Her research interests are Caribbean migration and its impact on national and organizational development, mental health, Diaspora, and the building of teams in the workplace. She has published in academic journals and newspapers and is the author of the book *White Squall on the Land: Narratives of Resilient Caribbean People*. Hope Road Publications (London).

Tony Talburt is a lecturer in the Centre of African and International Studies at the University of Cape Coast, Ghana. He completed his B.A. degree in History and Social Science at the UWI, Mona and his M.A. in International Studies at the University of Warwick before completing his Ph.D. in International Politics and Development at the South Bank University, London in 2001. Tony Talburt is the author of *Rum, Rivalry and Resistance: Fighting for the Caribbean Spirit* Hansib Publications (UK) and he runs a consultancy in Birmingham, England.

Tarik Weekes is a Saint Lucian currently employed as a research officer with the Mona Social Services at the UWI, Mona. He has worked extensively in Jamaican communities in areas of community development needs and violence prevention. Prior to joining Mona Social Services, Weekes served as a coordinator and researcher for the Kingston West Crime Observatory spearheaded by the Violence Prevention Alliance - Jamaica Chapter. In 2012, he started the Gang Mapping Project with the goal of strengthening the availability of data on gangs operating in the country and the need for social development in inner city communities. Tarik Weekes is also pursuing doctoral studies with a focus on assessing special projects in policing that target gang related murders.

Basil Wilson is provost emeritus of John Jay College of Criminal Justice at the City University of New York. Presently he is the executive director of the King Research Institute at Monroe College, Bronx, New York and a professor in the Master's Programme in Criminal Justice. His research interests include urban violence, globalization, poverty in urban communities, and understanding homicide rates from a comparative perspective.